The

Guide to Baby's First Year

Essential Information, Practical Advice and Key Choices for Your Baby's First 12 Months

Jamie Loehr, M.D. and Jen Meyers

SOURCEBOOKS, INC.
NAPERVILLE, ILLINOIS

Published by Sourcebooks, Inc.
P.O. Box 4410, Naperville, Illinois 60567-4410
(630) 961-3900
Fax: (630) 961-2168
www.sourcebooks.com

Cataloging in Publication data is on file with the publisher.

Printed and bound in the United States of America.
BG 10 9 8 7 6 5 4 3 2

Contents

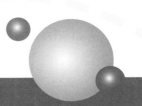

Part Three: Hot Topics 127

Dedication

For my love, Stevan.
And my souls: Riley, Torin, and Cael.
—J.M.

For my family:
Devon, Kieran, Shannon, and Mariah.
And most of all, Caitlin.
—J.L.

Acknowledgments

There are so many people to thank, more than we have mentioned here, but we wanted to share our appreciation of a few individuals who have helped us during the writing of this book. Our thanks go to our editor, Ewurama Ewusi-Mensah, whose comments, insights, and editorial skills strengthened the book, and to Grace Freedson, our wonderfully supportive agent. We'd also like to thank Leslie Daniels for support as we started this project, and Cheryl McLeod, Sandra Busby, and Kim Schindler for sharing their knowledge and experience. Special thanks to Diane Weissinger, the best lactation consultant in Ithaca, and to Caitlin Loehr for her expert editorial suggestions. Thanks to all the parents and children we have known over the years who have helped shape our knowledge and experiences.

Our parents deserve thanks—Rick and Pam Meyers, and Joan and Ray Loehr—simply for being our fabulous parents.

To our families, though, go our biggest thanks. Their support, good humor, and love during the writing of this book made it all possible. Thanks to Caitlin, Devon, Kieran, Shannon, and Mariah Loehr. Thanks to Stevan, Riley, Torin, and Cael Knapp. We love you!

Introduction

Welcome to your baby's first year! You are embarking on the most amazing journey of your life—becoming a parent, raising a child. Parenthood. Truly the toughest job on Earth, and easily the most rewarding. Sit down, lace up your hiking boots, and get ready for a wild trip.

Like all journeys, there will be ups and downs. There are some maps, but you will often have to decipher the key. Parenting is hard work, incredibly demanding, and abundant with unconditional love. For some of us, it may be the first time in our lives that we feel this kind of love.

Parenting is never boring because it is always changing. (It can be incredibly frustrating, but it's never boring!) You learn as you go. As a parent, you will be continually evolving because your child will be constantly growing and changing. So what works today, may not work tomorrow. You'll have to figure out what will work. Again. And again. And again.

This book is comprised of our knowledge and experiences, as well as that of many parents we know. Our advice is based on what we have seen work well. While reading this book, you are going to come across lots of suggestions and advice. In the end though, remember three things:

1. Every baby, every parent, and every family is different.
2. *You* are the expert on *your* baby.
3. You make the final decision.

Our job is to give information and opinions; your job is to decide what to do with it. Though we hope most of our suggestions will be helpful, some may not work for you. No worries. If one suggestion doesn't work, try another. If our advice doesn't resonate with how you want to raise your baby, don't take it. As a parent, you will get lots of advice that you try out and plenty that you do not follow. You will learn what you want to do with your baby and what you do not want to do—by reading books and articles, by observing other parents, and by living day to day with your family.

In the end, you need to feel secure in the fact that you know your baby better than anyone else. You will know what works. You will know what doesn't work. You will know when all is well. You will know when something is wrong. Follow your gut. Follow your instincts. Trust yourself in this new role. Yes, maybe you've never done this before, but you still are the expert on *your child*. You have within you everything you need to do this. You are the final authority.

We hope that this book not only gives you information of what to expect during your baby's first year, but the power that comes from being informed. Knowledge is power. We hope to empower you to make decisions on your own rather than relying on someone else (like your doctor) to make them for you.

So, congratulations on joining the parenting club! And welcome! We wish you the journey of a lifetime.

Jen and Jamie

Part One

Preparing for Your Baby

Let's get ready for the arrival of your baby! We'll cover the issues that arise before your delivery, during your delivery, and in the first few days after your delivery. The most important of these is choosing a doctor for your baby. You will be entrusting your baby to her care, and you need to feel comfortable with her. Chapter One—Finding Dr. Right—includes a number of suggestions to help you match your personality and values with those of your baby's doctor and make sure you have a good fit.

Chapter Two enters into the world of baby paraphernalia, describing the things you need, things you might want, and things that you can probably do without. Then it is on to your delivery and hospital stay in Chapter Three. There are a lot of baby logistics that occur in the hospital—pokes and prods that you want to be prepared for. While some of them are mandated, others require your permission, and learning about them beforehand will help you decide your position on them before your baby is born.

Finally, in Chapter Four we discuss the first few days at home with your baby. You will begin to bond with your baby as you adjust to your new life at home, and we give advice for making this sometimes chaotic time a bit easier. This chapter also discusses sleeping arrangements that you need to consider, and instructs you how to ensure the safest sleeping environment for your baby.

So let's go!

Finding Dr. Right

A good pediatrician is worth her weight in gold . . . okay, more like two or three times her weight! Having a doctor whom you trust to provide exceptional care to your baby is incredibly important. You'll need to think about what kind of doctor you want and what kind of relationship you hope to have with her. The best way to do this is to come up with a list of qualities you hope your baby's doctor will have. Start looking *before* the baby arrives. Your OB or midwife will expect you to have a pediatrician ready to come examine your baby in the hospital or birth center after he is born.

This may strike you as a bit of a challenge because, like many new parents, you probably do not know any pediatricians. In addition, many first-time parents do not have friends who have children, so it may seem as if there's no one you can ask for recommendations. Regardless, there are a number of things you can do to find the right doctor for your baby.

In this chapter we'll prompt you to think about what you feel is important in a doctor. We'll provide ways to find a doctor and questions you'll want to ask in an interview. Hopefully, you'll decide what qualities are uniquely important to you, and learn how to find the perfect doctor for your baby.

The List of Doctors

First consider what kind of physician you want. You are not limited to just pediatricians when looking for a doctor for your child. Family physicians also care for children. In fact, some family physicians also deliver babies!

A note from Jamie . . .

Many patients of my practice appreciate having only one doctor take care of them and their babies before, during, and after birth. There's a nice continuity, and a family doctor can care for the rest of the family as well. I have some four-generation families in my practice—so I am caring for great-grandparents, grandparents, parents, and the new baby!

Both pediatricians and family physicians can provide equally excellent care for your child. The bottom line is that you want someone you can trust—someone you feel really knows and cares about your child as an individual and who respects you and your instincts as a parent.

So how do you find a pediatrician or family doctor? You can always open up the phone book or your insurance book to find a list of doctors, but the best way is to ask around. And the best sources are people with children, of course. Talk to moms and dads at the grocery store, playground, library, mall—wherever you see them. Parents who have a good doctor will be happy to tell you about her. If you have friends or family members with kids who live near you, ask them. Ask your obstetrician or midwife for recommendations. Ask your chiropractor. Ask your dentist. Ask your coworkers. Go to a La Leche League meeting and ask people there. (La Leche League is an international nonprofit organization that is recognized as an authority on breastfeeding.) You get the idea! You are sure to come away from all this with a solid list of possible doctors to interview.

The Interview

Before you meet with or call your prospective doctors, take some time to come up with a list of questions to ask. Think about what will be important to you as a parent, the qualities the doctor must have, and ideas and plans for care that you must have in common. We are going to present you with a good number of questions to consider. Choose the ones that are important to you and limit your interview to those questions. You do not need to ask the doctor every question we list here—unless, of course, they are all important to you.

Also, think about what kind of relationship you want to have with your doctor. Do you want to make decisions yourself or just follow expert advice? Are you looking for a partner in your child's care or do you want the physician to be the "captain of the ship" with final responsibility at the end of the day? We are of the belief that parents should think, question, and ultimately decide all things in the care of their children, and we have formulated the questions that follow based on that belief. You may feel differently. That's perfectly fine. It's something you need to consider when choosing a doctor.

Finally, keep in mind that you may not be able to tell everything about the doctor when you interview her. There are some questions to which you might not be able to get answers—such as how well the doctor interacts with children—until you bring your baby to see her.

The following is a list of the questions and qualities we feel are important to consider when looking for a physician for your baby. We hope they will inspire you to come up with further questions or issues you may not have thought about before. You may notice that we didn't include any questions about the doctor's background, such as where she went to medical school, how long she has been in practice, or any special training she might have. In our experience, those issues aren't that relevant. A great doctor might be fresh out of training or have been in practice for forty years. We feel that the quality of care she provides your child and how you relate to her is more important than whether she trained at an Ivy League institution. However, as with anything that's important to you, ask it if you feel it's significant.

Questions to Ask the Nurse or Office Staff

✓ What are the office hours?

✓ Will the doctor be available to see me in the evenings or on the weekend, if necessary? How are after-hours calls handled? Do the on-call doctors have beepers or an answering service? Does the practice use an answering machine that is checked periodically by the doctor on call?

✓ Will I see the same doctor for every well-child visit?

✓ How quickly can my child be seen if sick? Will I be able to get in the same day I call?

✓ How long will I usually have to wait to see the doctor when I arrive for my appointment? Is the doctor typically overbooked?

✓ Is there a lactation consultant on staff or is there someone to whom the doctor regularly refers patients?

✓ Is it easy to find parking? (It can be really frustrating to have to search for a parking space when you are trying to get to a doctor's appointment—especially if your baby is crying in his car seat.)

Questions to Ask the Doctor

✓ Are you supportive of breastfeeding? What are your recommendations for breastfeeding? Do you support extended breastfeeding (breastfeeding beyond one year)?

✓ What sort of resources can you point me to in order to educate myself? Do you have books, websites, or community groups to recommend?

✓ (If you are not going to circumcise) Do you know how to care for a boy with an intact foreskin? Do you have much experience with it? Because many doctors do not have much experience with this, it is also best for you to educate yourself on how to care for an uncircumcised penis. That way you can educate your doctor, if need be, and protect your son from unnecessary pain.

✓ What is your comfort level with selective vaccinations? Which vaccinations would you feel most comfortable skipping? If you are not sure about vaccinations—perhaps you want to delay some of the shots or are considering not vaccinating at all—you should definitely bring it up in the interview. Many doctors will not accept your baby as a patient if you do not vaccinate. It is best to get that issue out in the open from the start.

> It's important for you to have a good understanding of your child and his development, so finding a doctor who can encourage you in that direction is key. If she only suggests handouts or tells you not to bother doing your own research, make sure you feel comfortable with that attitude. Personally, we feel strongly that you should be in a partnership with your child's doctor. You want someone who will listen to you and trust you as an authority on your child. You do not want a dictator.

✓ Do you have children?

✓ If you have special dietary concerns or restrictions in your household (such as a vegetarian or vegan diet), you may want to ask how the doctor feels about children following that diet and what kind of experience she has with it, as well as recommendations she's able to make for keeping the diet healthy.

Things to Observe and Questions to Ask Yourself once You've Begun Seeing the Doctor

- Does the doctor enjoy working with children? Does she interact well with kids?
- Do you feel rushed when you get in to see the doctor for either a well-child or a sick visit?
- Does the doctor treat you like an intelligent person or brush off your opinions and concerns?
- Does the doctor listen to you?
- Does the doctor appear to trust that you know your child and that you know when something isn't right?
- Do you feel relaxed with the doctor or do you feel rushed and pressured? Does the doctor give you her full attention or is she only half listening?
- How far away is the doctor's office from your home? Is it important to you to have a doctor who is fairly nearby? If you find a great doctor, would you mind if her office was 45 minutes away?

Think about these questions. Did you think of any others when you read the list? Write them down. Make a list of questions that touch on issues that are important to you so you will not forget to ask them when you interview a potential doctor. Choose the questions from this list that you feel are relevant and add them to your own list. You do not want to bombard a doctor with question upon question upon question—your interview may last only five or ten minutes. That's usually enough to get a feel for who the doctor is and whether you think she'll be a good match for you and your family. But remember: you are interviewing these doctors to work for *you*—to take care of your child.

If you have a choice, an interview in person is always better than a phone interview. However, you should know that not all physicians' offices encourage interviews, and some may charge for them. (If you have insurance, you'd pay your co-pay as if it was a regular doctor's visit.) Also, if someone has a great reputation and doesn't accept interviews, she still might be worth checking out. You can ask your questions during the first visit.

Lastly, keep this in mind: The doctor you choose now is not necessarily forever. If you realize that you do not like the doctor or the practice after all—for whatever reason—you can always find another physician later on.

One More Thought . . .
When you interview a doctor, if you like her but do not agree on all issues, don't dismiss her outright. Though you may not agree on everything, remember that you can take or leave the advice. The purpose of the interview is to get the doctor's opinion on certain issues and to get a sense of the doctor as a professional and as a person. Just because she may express an opinion that differs from your own doesn't mean she'll force her opinion on you or disregard your input. Give the relationship a chance to develop.

Perhaps you will get a great recommendation from a mom or dad in your new playgroup in a few months. This is one area in which you do not want to settle for less, so if you aren't satisfied with the care your child's doctor is providing, don't hesitate to take your baby elsewhere.

2

Baby Paraphernalia

Shopping for your baby is so exciting! Those adorable tiny clothes—little baseball caps, sunhats, dresses, snuggly snowsuits, blankets, teddy bears—so much to decide on! Figuring out what to buy for your baby can be a lot of fun, but with so many sources telling you all the "must-haves" in baby gear, it may also be overwhelming. If you are able to afford anything and everything, then you can get all the basics plus the bells and whistles, too. If, like us, you have to watch your budget, then you need to know which items are essential or useful and which are just luxuries or downright unnecessary. Although we cannot possibly create a comprehensive list of every single baby item available, we have done our best to give you information that can help you decide what you want to have for your baby.

What to Consider

Before you even step into a store or surf the Internet, you need to think about your lifestyle and environment. Consider the following:

* Where do you live? In the suburbs, the city, the country?

- Will you be walking to places with your baby? Will you drive?
- Do you plan to jog or walk for exercise? Are there trails you might walk?
- Do you live in a house or an apartment?
- How much space is there in your home?
- Do you plan to carry your baby a lot?
- Do you have a washer and dryer in your home or do you go to a Laundromat?
- Is your baby going to sleep in her own room or in your room?
- What time of year will your baby be born?
- What is the weather like where you live?

How do these things affect what you need for your baby? Well, if you live in a one-bedroom apartment, you probably do not want to fill the place up with bulky baby equipment like high chairs, swings, and changing tables. You most likely won't have the space for those things. If you don't ever walk anywhere, you probably won't need a stroller. If you do your laundry once a week in a Laundromat, you might want to buy extra clothes and sheets. Take some time to think about whether you will use each baby item before you buy it.

If you will be filling out a registry so friends and family will know what items you'd like to have, try to be as specific as possible about what you need or want. For example, you might want specific brands or models, such as a highly recommended car seat or a specific style of diaper bag. You know yourself, your lifestyle, and your needs better than anyone. Registries make shopping easier for the people who will be buying gifts for you and your baby, and they're a great way to make sure that you'll get exactly what you want. Of course, if you get gifts that aren't quite right for you, you can easily take them back to the store. Knowing exactly what you need ahead of time will help you decide what to keep and what to exchange or return before your baby arrives.

The Essentials

The items on this list are the basics that you'll need when your baby is born. Some things you will need right when the baby arrives, but others can be purchased later on (see page 17).

Things You'll Need Right Away

✓ Car seat

✓ A place for baby to sleep

✓ Sheets and blankets

✓ Mattress protectors (a large covering to protect the mattress from diaper leaks)

✓ Lap pads (smaller coverings to protect you or small areas from diaper leaks)

✓ Clothing

    Onesies (12)

    Sleepers (6–8)

    Hats (2–3)

    Socks (5 pairs)

    One-piece outfits (5–6)

    Sweater

    Blanket sleepers (3, if it's cold at night where you live)

✓ Receiving blankets (4+)

✓ Diapers

✓ Diaper pail (if you're using cloth diapers)

✓ Wipes

✓ Diaper bag

✓ Diaper rash cream or ointment

✓ Baby wash (unscented soap)

✓ Baby wash cloths (8–10)

✓ Dresser for baby's clothes (can also be used as a changing table)

✓ Snowsuit or bunting (if baby is born in the winter and you live in a cold climate)

✓ Thermometer (Do not use mercury thermometers which can be toxic if broken.)

✓ Infant nail clippers, small emery boards (nail files), or scissors for trimming baby's nails

✓ If you are breastfeeding:

Nursing pads (6–10) (they absorb breast milk so it won't leak onto your shirt)

Nursing bras (start with 2–3 to find out which you like best)

✓ If you're not breastfeeding:

Formula (1–2 cans)

Bottles (6–8)

Nipples (6–8)

Bottle brush

Car Seats

If you will be traveling in a car with your baby, you will need a car seat. In the United States and Canada, child passenger safety laws require car seats for infants, and you should use a rear-facing carrier infant seat for the first full first year of life—regardless of your child's weight or height. Car seats have a variety of different features that can help make the process of safely transporting your baby easier. Many seats come with a detachable base that stays in the car (or cars if you buy an extra base). The seat snaps into the base, meaning you don't need to adjust seat belts every time you go somewhere with your baby. The carrier function is also nice for moving a sleeping baby from the car into the house without waking her up.

There are a variety of sources that review car seats and offer comments on safety, ease of use, and features. A good starting resource is *Consumer Reports*, which can be found at your library or online (www.consumerreports.org), but there are plenty of other sites that review car seats as well. Do your research before you shop, so you will know exactly what you are looking for in a car seat and can find the best price either locally or online. To find multiple sites that offer reviews of car seats, use an online search engine and type in the words *car seat reviews* or a similar phrase. (The best we've found beyond *Consumer Reports* are the National Highway Traffic Safety Administration at http://www.nhtsa.dot.gov/CPS/CSSRating/ and Consumer Search at www.consumersearch.com.) For those without access to the Internet, a great source of comprehensive car seat reviews is the most up-to-date edition of *Baby Bargains* by Denise and Alan Fields.

Sleeping Arrangements

Babies sleep a lot, and it's nice to have options for where you can put your baby down to sleep. One option is buying a sidecar for your bed or using a crib with one side removed. A sidecar is a bed that attaches to the parents' bed. It keeps your baby within reach, without actually having her in your bed.

If your baby will be sleeping in her own bed, you have a few options. You can buy a

> **Your diaper bag doesn't have to be a "diaper bag" bought in the baby department. It can be a tote bag, backpack, messenger bag, or any other kind of bag, as long as it holds what you need. You will get a lot of use out of it, especially if it's something you can keep using for toys, snacks, or other things to keep your child busy after he graduates from diapers. Make sure it is comfortable and easy to carry.**

standard crib with a mattress, a bassinet, or a portable crib. If you choose not to buy a crib, you can just purchase the crib mattress separately after baby outgrows the bassinet or portable crib. (If you are buying any of these items used, make sure they meet the updated safety standards. See Chapter Eleven for more details.) A portable crib is great to use if you do not have a lot of space in your

If you will be using a portable crib only when you visit family or friends, it's a good idea to have baby sleep in it a few times in your home. That way it will be a familiar place to her when she's in unfamiliar territory, and she'll be more likely to settle down to sleep.

home. It's much smaller than a standard crib, and it's easy to move around. Depending on how big your baby grows in the first year, you may not even need to buy a crib mattress. You may be able to jump right up to a big bed with side guards or just a regular mattress on the floor. (See Chapter Four for more information about safe crib sleeping.)

You'll need sheets and a couple of blankets for your baby's bed. Also, to reduce the amount of laundry and bed changing you'll be doing, it's essential to use a mattress protector or a lap pad. Placing a lap pad underneath baby in your bed or her bed means that if she spits up or her diaper leaks, you will only need to toss the lap pad in the laundry, not change the sheets and mattress pad on the bed. (This can happen on a daily basis—even a few times a day.) You can also use the lap pads when you change your baby's diaper, so that if she pees or poops while you're changing her—or if her diaper has leaked and is really messy—you will only need to wash the pad.

If you're going to use disposable diapers, you can wrap up the soiled diapers in plastic grocery bags. You do not need to buy special bags or fancy diaper pails. Now you'll finally have a good use for all those grocery bags piling up in your kitchen!

Diaper Matters

If you're considering using cloth diapers, your best bet is to research your options and purchase your diapers online.

There are many different kinds of cloth diapers—the classic flat-fold diapers, all-in-ones (which are like disposables in that they are just one piece), and variations in between. Do an online search with the words *cloth diapers*, and you'll find everything you need to know about diapering, as well as a plethora of sites with them for sale. If you plan to wash them yourself rather than using a diaper service, you'll need to have a washing machine in your home. Otherwise, you'll be visiting the Laundromat several days a week just to wash your diapers.

You'll also need a place to put the soiled diapers until they are ready to be washed. A bucket with a lid or a small garbage can with a lid works well. A washable liner that you can wash with the diapers helps contain the ammonia smell that comes from three-day-old diapers and it helps keep your container clean. (For more information on diapering—disposable and cloth—see Chapter Four.)

> **One thing to remember: babies who are exclusively breastfed do not have smelly poop. So you actually won't need to worry about stinky diapers for about six months if you're breastfeeding your baby!**

Things you'll need around four to six months

- Drool bibs (you can't have too many of these if your baby drools!)
- Food bibs (5–6)
- Baby-proofing items
    - outlet plugs
    - gates for stairs or to block off certain rooms

Bibs

You cannot have too many drool bibs if your baby is a drooler. (Drool bibs are smaller cotton bibs made for soaking up all that dribble!) Some babies do not drool much, so it's worthwhile to wait until the waterworks start; that way you won't stock up only to discover you don't need them. You'll also want to get some food bibs to protect baby's clothes from getting stained while she's learning to eat. If you do not mind stained bibs, cotton works just as well, though you'll want food bibs to be a little larger than drool bibs so they protect a larger area of clothing. Plastic and vinyl bibs are also available. Use whatever works. You'll eventually want to get some bibs that have a pocket to catch food that falls, so you won't have to wipe off or change your baby's pants after every meal.

If you do not want your baby wearing stained bibs all day long, then you'll want to have separate drool and food bibs. The drool won't stain the cotton bibs, but the baby food sure will. Baby food stains clothes very easily, so unless you wash each bib right away (and you're not likely to have time to do that), your cotton bibs will get covered with stains.

Remember that bibs are meant to protect your baby's clothing; they aren't meant to be kept pristine. Do you really want to stress about the bibs staying neat and clean? Better to relax and let baby make a mess during meals—it's inevitable.

Baby-Proofing Devices

In terms of baby-proofing items, the most important things you'll need are the outlet plugs and gates to block off stairs and rooms that you do not want your baby venturing into. You might want to get cabinet locks as well, but depending on the types of handles on the cabinet doors, an equally effective and much cheaper alternative may be to use strong rubber bands to keep them closed. (See Chapters Eight and Nine for more information on baby proofing.)

The Useful Items

Beyond the essentials that you'll need for your baby, there are many things that can help make life a bit easier. They include:

- ✓ Burp cloths (cloth diapers also work)
- ✓ Changing table cushion (just the cushion)
- ✓ Baby monitor
- ✓ Rocking chair
- ✓ Carrier (sling, frontpack, or backpack)
- ✓ Stroller
- ✓ Portable crib (and sheets)
- ✓ Crib mattress (and sheets)
- ✓ Baby towels
- ✓ Baby bathtub
- ✓ Bouncy chair
- ✓ Swing
- ✓ Vaporizer
- ✓ High chair or booster seat

About the Usefuls

Burp cloths become an essential if your baby spits up every time she eats. They will save you from having to change your shirt multiple times throughout the day, and save the clothing of the friends and family who hold your baby, too. If there's only occasional spit-up, burp cloths will be useful, but are not a must-have. There is no reason to buy specific burp cloths, you can use any kind of cloth—hand towels, dish towels, cloth diapers—basically anything that is cotton so it will be soft against your baby's face and quickly soak up any spit-up.

A baby monitor becomes really useful during naps and when baby is older. The American Academy of Pediatrics (AAP) recommends that babies sleep near their parents (in the same room) for the first year, so if you follow that suggestion you will not use it at night. A monitor may come in handy during the day when baby is sleeping if your house is big, or if you'll be going outside while she's sleeping inside. However, if you live in a small apartment, it's unlikely that you'd need a monitor. Once baby is older and sleeping in her own room, the monitor is an essential thing to have.

Babies love motion, and sometimes fall asleep more easily that way, so a rocking chair can be a real blessing to tired moms and dads. Carriers, whether they're slings, frontpacks, or backpacks, can serve a similar purpose—to get baby to sleep while mom or dad walks around or even works around the house. Carriers have the added benefit of giving mom and dad free arms to do stuff, whether it is yard work, the dishes, or working on the computer. Some babies will sleep better (and longer) if they are held, and carriers allow you to hold your baby asleep or awake and still be able to do things.

If you'll be walking a lot with baby, you may also want to consider buying a stroller. Depending on where you live and where you plan to walk, there are different types of strollers and you can find one that will fit your specific needs. Umbrella strollers— the simple kind that fold up like umbrellas—are for older babies, and are not a good choice for newborns. Some infant car seats can snap right onto a regular stroller, which is nice because you won't have to disturb your baby to put her into the stroller if she's fallen asleep in the car. You can just transfer her car seat to the stroller. If you will be walking trails in the woods or live in a rural area and go for walks, your best bet would be a jogging or all-terrain stroller. The same goes for if you'll be jogging or walking for exercise (as opposed to just meandering). This is another item that is best researched on the Internet before going shopping. You'll find reviews and vendors online if you do not have a good selection locally. You can also find good information about strollers in the most recent edition of Denise and Alan Fields' book *Baby Bargains*.

To make bath time easier, consider baby towels and a baby bathtub. The towels have a hood, which helps keep baby warm when she's being dried off. (A warm baby is a happy baby right after a bath!) Or you can easily use your regular towels and just be sure to put a hat on her right after her bath. A baby bathtub is helpful because it allows one person to wash baby in a sink. Of course, it's only useful for a few months, until baby grows too big for it. Another option is to simply place a folded towel in your bathtub, run just a little bit of warm water into it, and lay your baby down on the towel.

The Luxuries

A few items qualify as luxuries (though some people may consider them essential, depending on your preferences).
- ✓ All-terrain/jogging stroller
- ✓ Glider rocker
- ✓ Nursery decor
- ✓ Bottle warmer

The Unnecessaries

There are also a handful of things that we'd say are unnecessary.
- ✓ Changing table
- ✓ Wipes heater
- ✓ Shoes
- ✓ T-shirts
- ✓ Special diaper container and special bags for diaper disposal
- ✓ Baby oil
- ✓ Baby powder
- ✓ Walkers

About the Unnecessaries
A changing table is a completely useless piece of furniture once you're no longer changing diapers. You're much better off using a

concave changing pad on top of a dresser because you'll use the dresser for years to come. The only time a changing table might be useful is if your bathroom is big enough for one to fit there; it is convenient to change diapers next to running water and you can dump poop straight into the toilet. So if a friend offers you one for free, take it! You're sure to find changing tables at garage sales, too.

T-shirts are another thing to avoid. Stick to onesies because T-shirts ride up and expose baby's tummy. You'll spend all day pulling the shirt back down, which can be really annoying. Onesies are a staple in baby clothing. They can be worn alone when the weather is hot or as a layer when it's cold.

A fancy diaper pail that requires special bags is a waste of money. You get the same effect with a regular garbage can (one with a lid or without) and tying up the soiled diapers in a plastic grocery bag. You'll actually have a use for the hundreds of plastic bags in your pantry! What's better is that you get those bags for free every time you shop. No need to buy any diaper-disposing bags at all.

The final three items on our list are not only unnecessary, but can also be downright dangerous at times. Babies do not need baby oil or powder. Baby oil and baby powder, if inhaled or aspirated, can cause very serious damage to the lungs. Baby oil should be kept completely out of reach (in the medicine cabinet, for example) once baby is mobile. In fact, all oils should be kept out of reach. Cornstarch is a safer alternative to baby powder.

Walkers are also dangerous because babies can fall down the stairs when moving around in them. They do not help baby learn to walk any sooner and might even delay walking development, so they are not a very effective or useful piece of equipment either.

We hope this helps you sort out what you need and want to buy for your baby. Of course, there are many more items out there that we did not mention, but this list is meant to get you thinking about what you *really* need and help you decipher whether a product will be helpful or useless before you buy.

3

How to Plan Your Birth and Hospital Stay

The manner in which your baby is born can strongly influence his first weeks and months of life. Everyone wants their baby to have the best possible start. So to help you prepare, we're going to discuss a variety of issues that arise before, during, and in the first few days after the birth of your baby.

Different Birth Scenarios

You have choices when it comes to where your baby will be born. Some families deliver their babies at home, while others choose freestanding or in-hospital birth centers. We're going to focus on hospital births, simply because that is where the majority of families have their babies. We won't get into the pros and cons of various options but you should know that many of the topics discussed below are handled differently in these alternative settings. If you will be having your baby at home or in a birth center, please use this chapter as a springboard for discussing these topics with your midwife or physician.

Within the hospital setting, the two main categories of delivery are vaginal (including vacuum or forceps extractions) and Cesarean section (C-section). The C-section rate has climbed above 25 percent for most hospitals in this country, so you should be prepared for the very real possibility that you could undergo an operation to deliver your baby.

A C-section is quite safe overall, but it is still major abdominal surgery and should not be undertaken lightly. Statistically, mothers have a slightly increased risk of complications with a C-section as compared to a normal vaginal delivery. In addition, C-sections obviously lead to more pain, a longer recovery period, and more difficulty bonding with and nursing your baby. Thus while C-sections are occasionally necessary, we do not feel they should be routine. In other words, there should be a very good medical reason for a C-section, not just a physician or patient preference.

The best way to avoid a C-section is to prepare yourself for birth as much as possible. One of the most important things you can do is have excellent labor support from people you respect and trust. They could be family (husband, partner, parents, or siblings), friends, or even a well-trained labor nurse. Studies have shown that feeling safe, secure, and well cared for during your labor process decreases your need for pain medications and reduces your risk of vacuum or forceps deliveries or C-sections.

If you know you will be lacking such support at the time of your delivery, and you have the financial resources, consider hiring a *doula*. Doulas are trained professionals who provide you with emotional and physical support and encouragement during labor. Some even provide support in your home after your baby is born. You can often find a doula in your neighborhood by talking to your physician or midwife, chatting with other pregnant moms, or searching the Internet. A good starting point online is the organization Doulas of North America (www.dona.org) which allows you to search for doulas by city and state.

Another way to avoid a C-section is to not induce labor unnecessarily. Some inductions are necessary for the safety of the baby or mom. With some medical conditions, it is safer for the baby to be born, even born early, rather than stay in the womb any longer. However, many inductions are scheduled for the convenience of the parents or physician. Inductions usually involve "pitocin," a medication that stimulates the uterus to contract. While they usually go well, occasionally this artificially created labor pattern is more stressful for the baby than natural labor.

Just keep in mind that even if you do everything you can do to ensure a safe vaginal delivery, sometimes a C-section is not only necessary, it is lifesaving for both the mom and baby. Things don't always go as planned, and when that happens it's nobody's fault. It's just the way it is. The overall goal during labor and delivery is to have a healthy mom and baby, in whatever manner is necessary.

Your Birth Plan

The main role of a birth plan is for you to set out your preferences for labor. The birth of your baby will be one of the most memorable events of your life, and you should get to choreograph it as best you can. This is your chance to do things the way that you want, so dream big! If you feel most comfortable in a dimly lit room with orchestral music in the background and your partner holding your hand, by all means ask for that. As we mentioned above, whatever makes you feel secure, well loved, and well cared for, will also make your labor less painful and safer for you and your baby.

Remember, the overarching goal of the labor process is to end up with a healthy mom and baby. Thus, certain parts of your birth plan may need to be set aside in deference to your or your baby's well-being. Think of it as a guideline that will be followed if all goes well. Sometimes the unexpected happens, and you should be ready to do what needs to be done, even if it conflicts with your birth plan, to make sure everyone is safe. Don't become so wedded to the birth plan that you are unable to change directions mid-labor.

Having said that, it is also fair to say that many hospital routines and protocols in use today are set for the convenience of the physicians, midwives, and staff rather than the laboring mother, and some of them have questionable benefits when researched carefully. For example, standard fetal heart rate monitoring, in which you are attached to a monitor for hours at a time, is not necessarily the best care. For low-risk mothers with normal pregnancies, continuous fetal heart rate monitoring has been shown to increase the incidence of vacuum and forceps deliveries, as well as C-sections, without any benefit to the mom or baby. Alternatively, intermittent monitoring before, during, and after one contraction every fifteen to thirty minutes has been shown to have excellent outcomes with fewer interventions.

Another outdated procedure is routine episiotomy. An episiotomy is a cut made in your perineum to provide additional room for the baby to come out. In the past, episiotomies were performed in the vast majority of deliveries. Recent research has shown that an episiotomy makes the delivery about fifteen to twenty minutes faster, but with a much higher risk of more extensive tears. There are times when it is critical to deliver the baby sooner and those fifteen minutes might be lifesaving for the baby. However, for normal deliveries, it is clearly better for you to tear on your own instead of having an episiotomy.

In the end, we want you to recognize that delivering a baby is a natural process that has been extensively medicalized. Certainly there are benefits to that change in focus, and some babies are born now who would have died in the past. However, there are also negative consequences. Many other countries have lower C-section and intervention rates without any increased complications to the mother or baby. So beware of following policies and protocols blindly without understanding the rationale behind them.

For parents, this is a very fine line to walk. On the one hand, you have to trust your provider. Remember, you are asking your physician or midwife to care for your most precious treasure—your baby. So if they say that something is needed, the tendency is to trust them and their experience. But at the same time, it is appropriate, and *important*, to be well-informed. We all want to be "good patients" and not rock the boat. And especially if you are a first-time parent, it may be hard to question the physician about other ways of doing things (which might require you to be confrontational). But it is your right to have your questions answered. You may feel like you are being a bother, but this is your life and your baby's life, and you are entitled to be as well-informed as you want to be.

When approaching sensitive topics, remember to phrase your questions with care and tread respectfully, asking for your provider's help in understanding your options and the possible reasons behind some routine procedures. You don't want to set your doctor on the defensive simply by the *way* you question her. Try to do your homework ahead of time, if possible. Find out what protocols and routine procedures are followed at your hospital (by asking your doctor during a visit), and then do some research to find out whether they are necessary for a low-risk pregnancy and delivery. If you are informed before talking with your doctor about issues that concern you, then you'll be better able to discuss them with her. And remember that you can revisit issues as you become more informed along the way.

Most physicians will be glad to help explain your options. If you find that your physician reacts poorly to your questions during your pregnancy, acts like you are bothering her, or gets defensive when you question her recommendations, it might be time to find another physician. It's never too late to switch doctors—the most important thing is that you are comfortable and confident in the provider who will attend the birth of your baby.

If you've had a baby previously, you are already a step ahead when preparing your birth plan. You can look back at your last delivery and think of things that you liked as well as things you wish had gone differently. In addition, if you have attended some-one else's delivery, you can use that experience to help write your birth plan. If you have any chance to attend a birth before your own, it is a wonderful opportunity to see the process up close and personal.

The best time to discuss your birth plan with your doctor or midwife is *before* you are in labor. You want to develop a trusting relationship before you are at the hospital, stressed, in pain, and exhausted. In the end, you want to trust your provider so much that if, despite your birth plan, your doctor feels a C-section or episiotomy is needed for the baby's sake, you believe her and are comfortable with her decision.

If this is your first labor, you will need other resources when writing your birth plan. Talk to friends and family members about their birth experiences and listen to any recommendations they might have for you. Ask other moms what was important in their deliveries and see if they have a birth plan you could see. Of course, you'll want to keep in mind that every pregnancy, birth, mom, and baby are different, so be sure to take in the information in the spirit of becoming well-informed and not necessarily as words to live by. In addition, many hospitals have preprinted plans available in their welcome packets. You can also do a search for birth plans online to get some great ideas. Use these resources as a starting point for questions to ask yourself and your midwife or physician.

A final note about birth plans: Occasionally, a very detailed plan is received with rolled eyes by the hospital staff. Labor is a variable process, and too much planning doesn't take into account the need to be flexible during that process. You should make a point of acknowledging that you recognize the need to be flexible and that you respect the expertise of the hospital staff. After all, you are relying on them to provide the best care for you and your baby.

This does not mean that you can't be firm about important issues. If it is a matter of staff convenience versus your well-researched and well-thought-out goals, feel free to push as to reach *your* goals. For example, we recommend spending as much time with your baby as possible, especially in the first hour of his life, and exclusively breastfeeding your baby if possible, so these might be inflexible guidelines to include in your birth plan.

Give a copy of your birth plan to your midwife or OB at one of your final visits, and pack several copies of it to take to the hospital or birth center. Give a copy to your nurse and keep some extras on hand if needed for the doctor on call, if your midwife or physician will not get to the hospital in time (that happens!) or if the nursing shift changes. You and your partner will be well-versed in your preferences and can voice them at appropriate times (when issues arise) if someone is uninformed. Ask for what you want. Speak up because it's the birth of your baby.

Sample Birth Plan*

We recognize that birth is a variable process and that the overriding goal is to have a healthy mom and a healthy baby at the end of the delivery. We also appreciate the experience and expertise of doctors and hospital staff.

If this is a normal delivery with a healthy baby at birth, these are the things we'd like to have happen:

1. Please explain all the pros and cons of suggested procedures to us, as well as any alternatives to the procedure.
2. We prefer intermittent fetal monitoring over continuous fetal monitoring, unless medically needed for the baby's safety.
3. Please do not offer any pain medications unless mom asks for them.
4. We would like to labor in the tub if it is safe for mom and baby.
5. We prefer no episiotomy unless needed for the safety of the baby.
6. Please delay all medical procedures for the first hour after birth. We want to have that time for just mom, dad, and baby to bond.
7. The baby will stay in mom's room throughout the hospital stay.
8. Mom will breastfeed baby, so no pacifiers or bottles, please.
9. If our baby is a boy, he will not be circumcised.
10. Thank you!

*This is just one example, and shouldn't be taken as a prescribed plan by the authors. Your preferences may be different, and that's fine.

Other Birth Issues

Group B Strep

Since 2002, the Centers for Disease Control and Prevention or CDC has recommended that all pregnant women be screened for Group B streptococcus (GBS) at 35–37 weeks of pregnancy. We are all familiar with strep throat, which is Group A strep. Group B strep is a related bacterium that causes no symptoms and has no significance unless you are pregnant. About 20 percent of women are carriers for GBS. If you are a carrier, your baby has a 1 in 200 risk of becoming infected with GBS during labor. The infection can be very serious for newborns.

To prevent the risk of infection, all women who are carriers for GBS should get an intravenous antibiotic during labor, usually penicillin. Studies show that if you have the antibiotic in your body for four hours, the risk for a GBS infection in the baby decreases to 1 in 5000. However, if you deliver before four hours have elapsed since the first dose of antibiotics, the risk is somewhere between 1 in 200 and 1 in 5000.

The important thing to know is that if your baby arrives before the four-hour mark, the CDC recommends that he stay in the hospital for at least forty-eight hours *and* have two blood tests to evaluate his risk for infection. In most cases, the first blood test, the complete blood count (CBC), will be normal and your baby will not need antibiotics. However, if the CBC suggests an infection, the physician might recommend antibiotics for two days while waiting for the final report from the second test (the blood culture) to come back.

Managing Pain in Labor

Labor is painful, but it is pain with a purpose—an amazing purpose! Just keep in mind that the discomfort is limited, lasts for a relatively short time, and is not unbearable—millions of women deliver babies each year without pain medication. But the pain can be severe, perhaps the most severe pain you will ever feel. So it makes sense for you to prepare for it.

As we stated above, the best way to start out is by making sure you feel safe, secure, and confident. Women who labor in the presence of loved ones, especially those who have been through the labor process before, are less anxious and more confident. They might not have less pain but they are better able to manage it. They also receive fewer interventions that might lead to complications with the delivery and thus complications with the baby.

In addition, there are many methods of relieving pain in labor other than medications. Laboring in water has been shown to decrease women's perceptions of pain, as well as the likelihood of interventions such as epidurals, vacuum extractions, and forceps deliveries. Instead of walking or sitting in a chair or leaning over on someone when you have a contraction, you are in a large tub of warm water. Other important options include changing positions in labor. Staying in the same position for long periods of time leads to additional aches and pain. Many women enjoy relaxing music and massage as well.

If you do decide that you would like additional help in dealing with the pain, there are different medical interventions available. The first choice is usually narcotic medications through an IV line. These will relieve mild to moderate labor pain and will also make you drowsy. However, if you have progressed to a more intense level of labor pain, IV pain meds are usually not sufficient. They tend to let you sleep between contractions, but when contractions do occur, you will wake up and feel them.

Since the goal of the pain meds is to relieve as much pain as possible, IV pain meds are not the right choice in the case of intense labor pain. In general, IV pain meds are useful for *prodromal*, or early, labor that is not severe—they allow you to relax and get some sleep. One drawback of IV narcotics is that they are frequently associated with a slowing of labor.

Another method of pain relief involves medicine given in the spine. There are two general forms: the *intrathecal* (also known as a spinal) and the *epidural*. Both involve inserting a needle into the spinal column and administering medications to certain areas of the spinal cord (the intrathecal or epidural spaces, respectively). The intrathecal has the advantage of providing more complete and more immediate relief but wears off in about one and a half to three hours. If labor is still continuing at that point, the intrathecal will have to be repeated.

The epidural procedure leaves a catheter in the mother's back. This allows the anesthesiologist to continuously drip medicine into the epidural space. It takes time to adjust the dose with an epidural, which leads to a slight delay in getting relief from pain. In addition, the epidural has a reputation of being "patchy" or giving incomplete relief. Some women report that a certain area is not fully relieved from pain. The epidural does not need to be repeated, though, and does not wear off, so it is more appropriate for longer labors.

Both the intrathecal and epidural have similar side effects. Almost all women notice *pruritus*, or itching over their body. This is annoying but tolerable. Other side effects are rare, but serious. Discuss these with your doctor.

So as you can see, there are upsides and downsides to using pain medications. They can have side effects, sometimes serious ones; however, pain medications can also help prevent complications. Sometimes women are too tense, too anxious, and too stressed by the pain to labor effectively, and relieving the pain allows them to have a safe vaginal delivery. In addition, some women appreciate the pain medications as a way to allow them to be more present at the birth of their child. They feel that if they are out of control due to the pain, they cannot fully experience the delivery as they would like. Consider your options carefully as you develop your birth plan, so you can help avoid making last-minute decisions on this matter.

After the Birth—The First Few Hours

Bonding with Your Baby

Congratulations on the birth of your baby! The next hour is one of the most special and most important in your life. It is a time to cry with happiness, be overjoyed, and be awed by your baby. Cherish this time. Hold your baby. Touch and kiss him. Count those beautiful little fingers and toes. Explore all the parts, the small hands and feet, the nose, the eyes. And when you and your baby are ready, nurse him.

Not only is it a wonderful feeling to spend the first hour with your baby, it is good science as well. Studies have shown that moms and babies who spend that first hour of life uninterrupted are more connected and have a better, more satisfying, and longer breastfeeding experience.

Unfortunately, hospital routines often interfere with that first hour of bonding. In some cases, those interventions are important. If your baby is not breathing well or needs stimulation, then whisking the baby to the warmer for more attention can be life-saving. However many of the routine interventions are for the convenience of the staff, physician, or midwife. For them, it is more efficient to get the necessary work done as soon as possible in case they are called to another delivery. Thus, the natural tendency is to try to do everything (baby exam, weight, eye ointment, Vitamin K, etc.) before letting you hold your baby, because as soon as their work is done, you can have him as long as you want. But it doesn't have to be that way. Most of these interruptions can wait until after you and your baby have spent the first hour of his life together.

Sometimes there are different or better ways to handle issues with your baby during that first hour than the interventions that hospital staff might suggest. If your baby is cold, don't just let the nurse put him under the warmer. A more effective (and enjoyable) way to warm him up is to snuggle skin to skin with mom or dad. Place him, wearing only a diaper, on your bare chest and wrap both of you up in a warm blanket.

Hospital Logistics, or What is Happening to My Baby?

Even if your baby is perfectly healthy, there are a number of interventions that occur in the hospital. It is important to understand that many of these recommendations come from the field of public health. Although your child may be at low or no risk of any of these infections or complications, in a country where four million babies are born each year, some babies are at risk. The public health point of view is that, by treating everyone, no one will get missed and everyone will be protected.

Eye Ointment

In the first hour of life, the hospital staff will put antibiotic eye ointment in your baby's eyes to protect against any unrecognized infection that can lead to blindness. Even though mom was likely checked for potential infections as part of prenatal care, most hospitals require this for all newborns.

Vitamin K

Another intervention in the first hour of life is a shot of vitamin K in the baby's leg. About 1 in 10,000 babies is born with a deficiency of vitamin K. This deficiency leads to a tendency to bleed more easily, especially in the brain. Hospitals give all newborns an injection of vitamin K as a preventive measure.

Hepatitis B Vaccine

Hepatitis B is a blood-borne virus that affects the liver. The most common methods of transmission include sexual intercourse, IV drug abuse, and blood transfusions, but it can also be spread by direct contact with infected blood or an open wound. Hepatitis B can also be transmitted from a mother to her baby during labor, presumably from the mixing of maternal and fetal blood during the delivery process.

If babies become infected with Hepatitis B during labor, over 90 percent of them become chronically infected, meaning that they carry the virus for the rest of their lives. More importantly, those children are at high risk of developing severe liver problems, liver failure, and liver cancer before the age of twenty.

Fortunately, research has shown that these dire consequences can be avoided with appropriate treatment in the first hours of life. For those children born to mothers already known to be carriers of Hepatitis B, giving the Hepatitis B vaccine and another product,

Hepatitis B Immune Globulin, markedly decreases their risk of becoming chronically infected. This treatment can be lifesaving for the baby.

However, even if a mother is not known to be a carrier for Hepatitis B, the CDC recommends that all newborn babies receive the Hepatitis B vaccine before leaving the hospital. Because there is a chance that the mother may be unknowingly infected, routine administration of the Hepatitis B vaccine ensures that no child is missed.

State Screening Exams

Every state has laws requiring that all babies be screened for certain serious but hidden medical issues. This test is often called the PKU test, short for phenylketonuria, which is just one of the disorders that the test detects. These screening tests are usually done by pricking your baby's heel and blotting his blood onto special paper that is sent to the state laboratory. It is vitally important to have this panel of tests completed because it screens for numerous problems that, if left undetected and untreated, can cause serious damage to your baby. If detected early, treatments are available.

A good example for understanding the purpose and limitations of this screening is the test for thyroid activity. About 1 in 4,000 babies are born with congenital hypothyroidism, or an underactive thyroid gland. In the past, these babies would not have been diagnosed until developmental delays were noted in the second year of life. Unfortunately, many of the delays had become permanent at that point. Today, however, when a baby's state screening exam shows below-normal thyroid hormone levels, the baby can be put on thyroid hormone therapy within the first weeks of life. With treatment he will develop normally with no delays.

Different states have different numbers of tests they run on babies' blood. Some states run as few as four, while others test for more than forty diseases. Most of the tests are for enzyme deficiencies or hormone imbalances. In some cases treatment requires a special diet, whereas with others certain medical care needs to be implemented immediately.

Another screening test done in some states is a hearing test. About 1 in 1000 babies is born with hearing difficulties. Several states have decided that it is better to diagnose this at birth instead of months later when the parents notice the child is not responding to voices. Early intervention with either cochlear implants or intensive sign language will help the child in the long run.

The hearing test is simple and safe, often done while the baby is sleeping and does not require any poking or prodding. It usually involves putting headphones on the baby's ears and then placing two sticky pads with electrodes on the scalp. A machine sends signals into the headphones and if the ears are working properly, the electrodes pick up the electrical signal transmitted from the ear to the brain.

As with the others, this test can also generate incorrect results that indicate the baby can't hear. Again, don't panic. More sophisticated follow-up testing later usually shows normal hearing.

> States set the levels of the tests to be extraordinarily sensitive. They do not want to miss anything, so they would rather catch all the abnormalities that indicate the possibility of disease than miss even one child with the actual disease. This means that the vast majority of abnormal results from the initial screen are not an indication of a medical problem at all and come back normal on follow-up testing.

Circumcision

Circumcision is the removal of the foreskin from the tip of the penis. In the United States, it is the most common surgical procedure performed, with over one million done every year. When looking at it from a global perspective, however, it is clear that circumcision is a culturally influenced procedure. Most European and Asian countries, for example, do not routinely circumcise their male children (with the exception of most boys born into the Jewish or Islamic faiths).

In the mid-1900s, more than 90 percent of boys born in the United States were circumcised. In 2003, the number averaged 55 percent, ranging from just over 30 percent in the West to just under 80 percent in the Midwest.

The most recent circumcision policy statement from the American Academy of Pediatrics Taskforce on Circumcision 1998–99 (reviewed and reaffirmed May 1, 2006) states in its Summary and Recommendations: "Existing scientific evidence demonstrates potential medical benefits of newborn male circumcision; however, these data are not sufficient to recommend routine neonatal circumcision." (http://aappolicy.aappublications.org/cgi/content/full/pediatrics%3b103/3/686.)

In other words, circumcision might have some medical benefits, such as preventing penile cancer in adult men, but those benefits are not significant enough to recommend circumcision to all boys. It would be like removing everyone's appendix to prevent appendicitis. This would certainly prevent many people from having appendicitis, but most people would agree the benefits of not doing routine appendectomies are clearly outweighed by the risks of universal surgery. Remember that circumcision is a surgical procedure that carries its own risks. You should discuss these with your doctor.

If you do opt in favor of having your son circumcised, insist on some form of pain relief. For years, physicians told parents that newborns didn't feel pain, or didn't feel pain in the same way that older children do. Subsequent research has shown that to be entirely untrue. Babies cry, have increased heart rates, elevated blood pressures, and other symptoms of pain in exactly the same way that older children and adults do. If your physician does not routinely provide pain relief with circumcision, insist upon it or find another physician to perform the circumcision. You wouldn't consider letting your child have surgery without pain medication; why should circumcision be any different?

There are multiple methods of pain relief for circumcision. These include topical anesthetic cream and/or a lidocaine injection like that used for dental procedures. In addition, adjunct methods of pain relief include allowing the baby to suck on a finger or pacifier coated with glucose water during the surgery, and using acetaminophen for the first 24 hours after the procedure. It is important to remember that you can use multiple methods, even all four methods at the same time. The goal is for your son to be more upset at having his legs strapped down on the procedure table than because of any part of the actual surgery itself.

Jaundice

Jaundice is the yellow skin color that occurs in over 70 percent of newborns in the first several days after birth. This color is due to a chemical called bilirubin, which comes from the breakdown of red blood cells. It is like the colors you might see in a bruise. When your skin is bruised, the red cells that make up the bruise break down and release bilirubin, which can give your skin a yellow hue a few days after the injury.

Babies are born with many more red blood cells than adults. After birth, excess red cells start breaking down and are reprocessed by the body. When the red cells break down, the bilirubin that is created is processed by the liver.

All babies will have some elevation in their bilirubin, but some have a much higher level than others. For example, some babies simply have more red cells, and thus have more red cells to break down. Some babies have inherited problems with their red cells that cause them to break down more easily. Occasionally, the liver takes a few days to get up to speed, thus delaying the body's ability to process the bilirubin. Each of these situations can lead to a higher than normal bilirubin level and jaundice.

Jaundice is just a reflection that the bilirubin is elevated, but it doesn't tell you how high. An extremely high level can lead to brain damage and long-term neurological complications. Unfortunately, the actual danger level varies, depending on how many hours old, how sick, and how premature the baby is. A five-day-old, full-term, healthy baby might not develop brain damage until the bilirubin level is over thirty, but a one-day-old, thirty-two-week, premature baby with a severe infection might have problems with a bilirubin of fifteen.

Fortunately, high levels of bilirubin are extremely treatable. The most common treatment is phototherapy. A certain wavelength of blue light penetrates the skin and helps the body process the bilirubin more efficiently. Light therapy usually lasts for one to three days until the liver can get up to speed processing the bilirubin on its own.

Another treatment for a high bilirubin level is to keep the baby well-hydrated. Babies who feed frequently pee and poop more often, both of which help remove bilirubin from the body.

Weight Loss

All babies will lose weight in the first few days of life, so you shouldn't panic when you see your baby losing weight on Days 2 and 3. Breastfed babies usually lose 6 to 8 percent of their birth weight. This might be six to twelve ounces depending on the baby's original weight. Babies growing on formula might lose less weight than breastfed babies, but they still can lose 5 percent of their birth weight. For nursing moms it takes two to four days for your milk to come in, but this does not mean that your baby is not receiving any nutrition when he breastfeeds. Up to that point, you produce colostrum, a thin blue liquid that provides calories plus antibodies for protection against infection.

On average, your baby's weight will hold steady on Days four and five, and then start increasing after that. In addition, once the baby starts gaining weight, he will only gain an average of one ounce per day. So if you do the math, you will find that it might take two weeks for the breastfed baby to regain his birth weight. *This is completely normal.*

Doctors tend to worry when the baby loses more than 10 percent of his birth weight. This usually happens when the mother and baby have nursing difficulties. It is not a major reason to panic, but it is certainly a wake-up call to get extra help with breastfeeding. Many hospitals have skilled lactation consultants who can help a mom and baby become a more efficient breastfeeding team and thus get more milk into the baby. If you are already home, ask your own doctor, your midwife, or your baby's doctor for suggestions about where to get assistance. One excellent resource is La Leche League, an organization of women dedicated to helping moms breastfeed their babies successfully. We also provide more breastfeeding tips in Chapter Eleven.

If your baby continues to lose weight despite everyone's best efforts, remember the first rule of infant nutrition, which is simply "feed the baby." A well-fed baby is happier, cries less, and has more energy for nursing. A dehydrated baby is sleepy, tired, and lacks energy for nursing. This is the time to add extra calories, using donated breast milk or formula, while your milk supply is improving. Remember to continue to nurse frequently and to always offer the breast *before* the supplements. Some moms also find it helpful to pump in between feedings as the extra stimulation makes their milk supply increase faster.

If you live in an area of the country where you can easily obtain breast milk from a human milk bank, use that before you use formula. Breast milk from a milk bank is more expensive than formula, around $3.50 per ounce, and requires a doctor's prescription, but is better than formula.

If that option is unavailable, some moms will obtain breast milk from friends who are nursing. This is a riskier proposition because it requires you to trust the donor when she says that she does not have any transmittable diseases. (The milk bank screens for all those problems before giving out the donated breast milk.) Some moms may be unaware they have been exposed to certain infectious diseases. However, if you have access to a trustworthy supply with which you feel comfortable, then fresh, locally donated breast milk is a great choice.

Formula is the third option to think about when deciding how to supplement your nursing baby. While in general we recommend breast milk over formula, a few days of supplementing with formula can also help add extra calories.

So, now it is time to take your newborn angel home. He has passed the hearing test, had his newborn screening done, isn't significantly jaundiced, and hasn't lost too much weight. The hospital staff has been wonderful and supportive and you feel recovered from your delivery—maybe not completely, but you are stronger and have more energy. You are ready to try parenting on your own at home.

The last issue before you take your baby home is making sure he fits in the car seat. You will find it much easier to bring the seat to your baby than to try and adjust the seat in the car. Read the installation manual carefully and make sure the straps are snug, snugger than you might think. You should just barely be able to fit one finger under the straps at his shoulders. Remember that babies should face backward in the car for the full first year of life. And with everybody strapped in, you're off! On to a new adventure—the next stage of parenting.

Coming Home: The First Few Weeks

4

Welcome home! And welcome to the world, sweet baby! Mom is still riding the high of having given birth, Dad still has that rush of adrenaline from the delivery, and your relatives and friends are reveling in the joy of having a new baby in the family. Despite all the excitement, we encourage you to pace yourself as you settle in with your beautiful little love. Slow down, rest, and take your time. This is the time to enjoy yourself by enjoying the baby. Sleep when your baby sleeps. Let the house get messy! The baby will only be this little once, so take the time to be with her and enjoy it as much as possible.

Life as You Know It
Your life is likely to feel chaotic at first because newborns have very unpredictable schedules. You may feel as if you can't get anything done and can't make plans because you have no idea what your baby's schedule will be like. Know that you'll all settle into a reliable and predictable routine by three to four months, with regular sleeping, waking, and feeding times.

Visitors

Most new parents are going to have many visitors in the first few weeks of their baby's life. Both friends and relatives want to see the baby and congratulate the family. But remember: A parent's job is to take care of the baby. Everyone else's job is to take care of the parents. Most visitors will be helpful and nurturing and keep their visits brief. You may find however, that some visitors drain your energy or expect you to play host. Limit the visits of these people—they only hamper what should be a positive experience for you and your baby.

Ask yourself who you want to see. Who will make you feel better and make your life easier? It is okay to politely decline visitors for awhile. Some families want to have the first two weeks to themselves before they allow any visitors at all. When you do have visitors, ask everyone to call before coming over. Don't feel guilty if you need to reschedule a visit or, heaven forbid, not show off the baby because she is sleeping. And try to keep visits brief. You are not hosting a dinner party; you are sharing your baby with the world.

The other important tip regarding visitors is to make sure everyone washes their hands. Everybody, and we do mean everybody, *must* wash their hands—either with soap and water or portable hand sanitizers—before they hold your baby. Hand sanitizers are more convenient than soap and get your hands just as clean, so they will probably be used more often. We recommend that you keep several bottles around the house as well as one in the diaper bag.

"Yes, That Would Be Lovely . . ."

Many people offer moms and dads help in the baby's early weeks of life, but all too often many of us decline help and try to manage on our own. Our advice is to learn to say, "Thank you very much.

That would be lovely." (If this is difficult for you, practice saying it to your reflection in the mirror until it comes out smoothly and easily!)

Any help you get means more time that you can spend with your baby. And accepting help gives you a feeling of being supported and celebrated, which is the way it should be. So, we say accept help graciously, and if anyone asks, be ready to make suggestions about what kind of help you need the most.

Some helpful things people can do for you include: bringing over a meal, shopping for groceries, walking the dog, having an older child over for a playdate, doing your laundry, folding clothes, sweeping the kitchen floor, or just holding the baby so you can take a shower. The list goes on and on. Don't be afraid to be creative when asking for help.

Diapering Your Baby

You've probably already made the decision about whether you will use disposable diapers or cloth diapers. But let's take a moment to go over the basics here. If you will be buying disposables, try different brands until you find the one that leaks the least on your baby. There is no one best disposable diaper. Some are fancier than others. Some have cartoon characters on them. But what it all comes down to is this: You want a diaper that will not leak. Different brands work best on different babies, probably due to their body shapes. Once you've found your favorite brand, shop around for the store with the best price! Stock up when they're on sale, and buy them in bulk when you can.

When it comes to sizing, follow the weight shown on the bag or box. Your baby should be at least at the lower end of the weight range for the diaper to fit her and not be too big. Remember to leave room in the diaper for baby's bottom to breathe. You don't want to have diapers that are too tight fitting (that results in more leaks—especially poop leaking). You'll usually find yourself moving up to the next size when baby's weight hits the middle of the weight range, which generally puts her at the lower end of the weight range for the next size up.

If you will be using cloth diapers and washing them yourself, there are a few steps to follow with a poopy diaper. If the poop is just watery, don't worry about it. Put it in the washing machine as is. If the poop has form or you can scrape it off, you can either rinse the diaper in the toilet or tie up the poop in a plastic bag and put it in the garbage—whatever works best for you. If you will be using a diaper service, they'll likely offer instructions on what to do with soiled diapers.

You'll probably wash diapers every other day. The best way to do that is to first run the diapers through a soak cycle on cold. Follow with a spin cycle to remove the debris. Then wash the diapers in hot water with a cold rinse, using only about one-quarter of the amount of laundry detergent you'd usually use for a load of clothes. Wash the diapers and diaper covers together, but wash baby's clothes separately. (The exception would be when baby's clothes get soiled with poop. Wash the soiled clothes with the diapers, and then wash them again in a clothes load.) Some parents have found that a second rinse cycle removes any soap residue and helps prevent rashes.

How to Change a Diaper

First, make sure you have all your supplies within reach:
- clean diaper
- wipes
- diaper rash cream (if needed)

Next, undo baby's clothes from the waist down.

Open the dirty diaper and remove it. (If your baby is a boy, cover his penis with a wash cloth or a clean cloth diaper in case he pees!)

Gently wipe baby's bottom from front to back, cleaning the area.

Place the clean diaper under baby's bottom.

If baby has a rash—any redness in the diaper area—slather on a thick layer of diaper rash cream. Use an extra wipe to get the leftover cream off your hands so it doesn't get on baby or her clothes.

Fasten the new diaper. (Tight enough to avoid leaks, but not uncomfortably tight.)

Snap up baby's clothes.

Dressing Your Baby

Many new parents wonder how to dress their baby. The simplest answer is that you should dress your baby in clothes that are similar to what you are wearing at the time but with one extra layer. So if you are wearing a long-sleeved shirt and long pants, your baby should wear the same plus a light sweater. If you are in shorts and a T-shirt, she should be dressed in shorts, a T-shirt or onesie, and maybe a light blanket.

As for how to actually get the clothes on your baby, the general rule to remember is "Head in first, out last." This means putting the clothing on over her head before covering her arms and taking the clothing off her arms before taking it off her head.

You also need to assess how hot or cold your baby is in various sets of clothes. Some babies seem to have higher or lower set points than others, and they feel hotter or colder than other people in the room at any given time. To assess your baby's temperature, do not rely on checking her hands or feet. They are often cooler than the rest of the body. Instead, rely on her head or chest to see how cold or warm she is. Many babies will have cool hands even when they are hot and sweating inside their sweater. A sweaty neck is a good sign that your baby is hot and needs fewer layers.

If you need to help your baby warm up, the best thing to do is to put a hat on her head. A baby's head makes up 25 percent of her body's surface area, while an adult's head is less than 10 percent. Thus, babies lose much more heat from their heads than adults and older children do. A hat quickly preserves some of that heat. If your baby seems too hot, removing her hat will help her cool down quickly.

Dressing your baby at night is more complicated. First, you want to keep the baseline house temperature high enough. Many families lower the temperature at night to sixty-four or even sixty-two degrees Fahrenheit. With an infant in the house, we recommend keeping the temperature above sixty-eight degrees. Second, remember that when your baby is sleeping, you need to protect her against suffocation, so comforters are not a good idea. At most you might put her down with a light blanket that reaches only up to her chest, not her face. It is better to keep her warm using pajamas with footies or a blanket sleeper than using an actual blanket or comforter. And don't put her to sleep with a hat on. Not only could she overheat, but if the hat twists in the night, it could lead to suffocation. (See the Sleeping Safely section at the end of this chapter for more information on keeping your baby safe at night.)

One last note on dressing your baby—if she has a fever, *do not bundle her up*. As adults, when we have a fever we tend to pile on the layers to keep warm. But that's very dangerous to do with a baby because it will actually make her fever rise, sometimes creating a dangerously high body temperature. When she's running a fever, keep her only lightly clothed, perhaps in only a onesie, pants, and light blanket when it's cold out or just a onesie or diaper when it's warm. Finally, if your baby has a fever during the first two months of life, call your doctor immediately, day or night. As we discuss in Chapter Sixteen, fevers in this age group usually require urgent evaluation.

Baths and Skin Care

Many parents ask, "Can I give my baby a bath?" Fortunately, newborns don't really need baths because they don't get very dirty. You need to clean their bottoms when they poop, but otherwise a simple washcloth with water in the creases and crevices of the body is sufficient until the umbilical cord falls off.

A common suggestion is to use alcohol wipes around the umbilical cord to keep it clean. While this is not harmful, it is also not necessary. Umbilical cords fall off on their own around two to three weeks after birth, sometimes as early as three days and, rarely, as late as six weeks. When the cord falls off, it will be very smelly, like an old scab finally coming loose, and will usually leave some crusted debris behind. At this point it is fine to use a cotton-tipped swab with petroleum jelly or ointment to clean the belly button and soften and remove the debris.

Once the cord is off, it is okay to give the baby an immersion bath. This is not required, but it sure is fun! And it makes for great pictures. Remember to be safe, though. Babies are slippery when wet and can easily slip from your grasp and dunk their heads under water. Many parents find it easier to give their baby a bath with a washcloth or towel wrapped around the baby to provide them with a better grip. You can use any soap and shampoo for the bath, although you may find that some, particularly baby soaps and shampoos, are gentler on the skin or less painful if they get in the eyes. If your baby has sensitive skin, it is fine to use no soap at all; water is sufficient. Make sure you have a cup or bowl handy to pour water over your baby as that makes rinsing easier.

You can bathe your baby as often as you would like, whether that is once a week or every day. Some children do have dry skin. This is more common in the winter, or when there is a family history of eczema, allergies, or asthma. In those cases, the issue is not how often you bathe the children, but what you do after the bath.

First, you want to pat the child dry, rather than rubbing her with a towel. Rubbing is rougher on the skin. Avoid allowing her to air dry, because evaporation overdries the skin. Next, immediately slather lotion on the areas of dry, cracked skin. This will seal in the moisture from the bath. Continue with lotion at other times of the day whenever your baby's skin begins to feel dry. An unscented lotion is best, especially for children with allergies or sensitive skin.

How Hot?

When running a bath for your baby, you want to make sure the water is warm enough that she doesn't get cold being in the bath, but not so hot that she's uncomfortable. Test the water temperature before you put the baby into the bath by using the inside of your wrist. If it feels cooler than your skin, make the water a little warmer. If it feels hot, add some cold water to cool it down.

If you had your son circumcised, continue to use petroleum jelly along the surgery site until the skin has healed completely and no raw skin is visible. This will usually occur within several days. The jelly will not only help the skin heal faster but will also prevent the raw areas from sticking to the diaper. If you have some small gauze squares available, you can use them to place the ointment along the penis and then leave them in place. The gauze then becomes a barrier between any poop and the healing skin, which will help to prevent infection.

If you did not have your son circumcised, the only thing you need to know is that you should *never* forcibly retract the foreskin. Not only is that painful for your baby but you might cause a serious condition where the retracted foreskin is unable to return to its resting state.

Most uncircumcised baby boys have foreskin that comes to a point at the tip of the penis, with a small opening for urine to escape. This opening will enlarge over several years until the foreskin can be easily retracted over the glans of the penis. If your son has excess foreskin, it is okay to gently pull it back just a little to clean out any stool that might be lodged among the crevices. However, you should only pull to the point where tension begins and no farther.

Also, be sure any medical personnel who handle your son understand that they should not retract the foreskin. Many are uninformed on how to care for an uncircumcised boy. Some doctors may tell you retraction needs to be done when your baby is a year old. Others may tell you that you are supposed to retract it regularly to clean your baby's penis. That is simply not true. Nor is it necessary to retract the foreskin should your son need a urinary catheter. There is *never* any reason to forcibly retract the foreskin.

There are a few bath safety matters that will be more relevant when your baby is older but are worth giving you a heads-up about now. First of all, *never leave a baby alone in water—not even for a second*. Babies can drown in just an inch or two of water. If you have started baby's bath and find it necessary to step away for a moment, wrap her in a towel and take her with you. Second, be careful where you give the bath. If you are using a sink, make sure that there are no electrical cords nearby from a hairdryer or a kitchen utensil, for example. Be especially aware of this when you are at someone else's house or vacationing where the house may not be babyproofed. A child could easily pull on a cord while wet and be electrocuted. Finally, the recommended temperature for the hot water heater in your house is 120 degrees Fahrenheit. Keeping the temperature this low makes it impossible to scald your child in the bath. Most hot water heaters are set at a higher temperature, sometimes as high as 180 degrees Fahrenheit, so you need to check and make the necessary adjustment.

Other Skin Topics

Parents often wonder what to do with their baby's fingernails. They are so small and delicate, yet they still leave scratches on her face when she hits herself with her hands. There are several options. You can file them with a nail file. You can even bite them with your teeth; this may sound odd, but many parents feel they have the best control this way. Finally, you can clip them with clippers. This probably works best but makes most parents nervous as baby's fingers are a moving target. If you use clippers, be aware that you will probably draw blood at least once in baby's first year. She will cry (and you might cry, too) but there will be no lasting damage. Just wash the cut with soap and water and watch for signs of an infection.

Wait until your baby is deeply asleep to cut her fingernails. You'll have a much easier time because she won't be moving her hands or clenching her fists while you're trying to trim her nails.

You might notice birthmarks in the first few weeks of life that you didn't notice in the hospital or that were not there at birth but developed later. (Even if they appear a few weeks after birth, we still call them birthmarks.) The most common birthmarks are *vascular*. Made up of tiny blood vessels, they show up as pink to red changes on the skin. On medium and darker skin tones, if vascular birthmarks are small, they won't be particularly noticeable; if they are raised, they will be a darker red. A *stork bite* is one or more red dots that appear on the nape of the neck, as though left by the stork that was carrying the baby during delivery. An *angel's kiss* is a similar patch, but on the upper eyelids. Both of these birthmarks get very red when the baby is hot or crying but are fainter at other times. They tend to disappear over the first two years of life.

Another common birthmark is the *Mongolian spot*, which is found near or on the buttocks. The skin is a bluish color and looks bruised. It has no significance at all and may or may not fade over time.

A small percentage of children will develop raised red birthmarks called *capillary hemangiomas*. They can be found anywhere on the body and will often grow to a very large size over the first six months of life. They will then stabilize and shrink over the next several years, finally disappearing and leaving a patch of discolored skin. Although they may appear problematic, it is tricky to remove them, and experts feel it is best to let them disappear on their own. The only exception to this rule is when the marks are in a crucial area such as an eyelid, where they might prevent normal vision development. They can be treated with lasers, steroid injections, and, rarely, with surgery.

Sudden Infant Death Syndrome (SIDS)

Sudden Infant Death Syndrome, usually referred to by its acronym SIDS, is the sudden unexplainable death of a baby under one year of age. It is rare for a baby to die from SIDS during the first month of life; the risk of SIDS is highest between two and three months of age, and then it decreases. No one knows what causes SIDS, nor how to protect against it completely. But there are things you can do to lower your baby's risk of SIDS significantly.

First, studies have clearly shown that babies sleeping on their backs have a lower risk of Sudden Infant Death Syndrome (SIDS) than babies sleeping on their stomachs. The side is also considered an unsafe position because it is unstable and a baby can easily roll over onto her tummy.

About six thousand babies a year died of SIDS before a public health campaign was instituted to recommend babies sleep on their backs. A few years after the campaign started, only three thousand babies a year died of SIDS. Given that about four million babies are born in the U.S. every year, this works out to decreasing the risk from 1.5 in 1000 babies to 0.75 in 1000 babies.

Back to Sleep

Always put baby down to sleep on her back. And if your baby will be in day-care or looked after by a nanny or babysitter, make sure that the childcare provider does the same. Babies should never sleep on their stomachs or sides.

Second, if your baby will be sleeping in her own crib, we strongly encourage you to place her crib in your bedroom for the first year, if at all possible. This recommendation comes from the American Academy of Pediatrics (AAP), which believes that having your baby nearby reduces the risk of SIDS. In addition, having your baby in your bedroom facilitates breastfeeding, which offers further protection from SIDS.

Remember to make sure your crib meets the most up-to-date safety specifications. If you plan to have baby sleep in a used crib, check that it is safe first. The crib slats should be no more than 2⅜ inches apart, and the headboard and footboard should not have any cutout designs. Wider set slats and cutouts are hazardous because baby's head could get caught in them. Use a firm mattress and be sure that there is less than two fingers of space between the mattress and the side of the crib.

Next, you don't want to place comforters on top of a baby. At most you want a light blanket pulled only halfway up your baby's chest. Because many of us are used to pulling blankets all the way up to our necks, it may seem like an unpleasant way to sleep; however, babies can sleep very comfortably this way if they are dressed warm enough at night, and it's safer. You also need to remove any pillows or soft objects like stuffed animals from the crib whenever baby is sleeping there, because they could block her breathing space. Also, watch for crevices and spaces between the bed and the wall where she might become entrapped. Babies can fit into smaller places than you might believe and then suffocate. And don't use unusual sleeping places such as a couch or a waterbed. Softer bedding creates a higher risk of SIDS.

Factors that Increase the Risk of SIDS
- **Baby sleeping on her tummy or side**
- **Baby sleeping on soft surfaces, such as a waterbed, sofa, quilt, comforter, sheepskin, or pillow**
- **Smoking during pregnancy and after baby is born (even smoking outside the house)**
- **Baby overheating**

Sleeping Safely

The following safety guidelines come from the National Safety Council and the AAP Task Force on Infant Sleep Position and Sudden Infant Death Syndrome. The guidelines have been revisited again and again as new information and new studies have revealed what is most effective for reducing a baby's risk of SIDS.

If someone else is taking care of your child, whether for an entire day or just a few hours, be sure to instruct them about the safe way to put your baby down in her bed. Do not assume that everyone knows and follows these guidelines. Don't even assume that daycare providers follow the guidelines—20 percent of SIDS deaths happen in childcare settings. It's in your baby's best interest to educate anyone who will be caring for her in how to help her sleep safely.

Reducing Risk of SIDS
Crib Sleeping Safety Information

ALWAYS

✓ Put baby down to sleep on her back.

✓ Use a firm mattress with a tight-fitting sheet.

✓ Keep baby's sleep environment empty. Remove pillows, comforters, stuffed toys, and any loose bedding from baby's crib. They are a suffocation hazard.

✓ Dress baby lightly and keep bedroom temperature comfortable.

✓ Use a light blanket, not a comforter or heavy quilt, if you wish to cover the baby while she sleeps.

✓ Keep a blanket, if used, pulled up only as high as baby's chest to prevent it from covering her face.

NEVER

✕ Put baby to sleep on a soft surface, such as a waterbed, sofa, comforter, quilt, sheepskin, pillow, etc.

✕ Use plastic bags, such as dry-cleaning bags, as mattress protectors.

✕ Place a crib next to a window. A child can become entangled in the cords of blinds or draperies, and screens cannot prevent a child from falling out a window.

✕ Overbundle baby. Overheating is a possible cause of SIDS.

✕ Smoke, during or after the pregnancy.

Crib Specifications

- The mattress should fit tightly into the crib—if you can get two fingers between the mattress and the sides of the crib, the mattress is too small and must be replaced.
- The crib slats should not be any wider than 2 3/8 inches apart.
- The headboard and footboard should not have cutout designs.
- The corner posts should be the same height as the end panels, or no more than 1/16 of an inch higher.
- If you use a bumper pad, it should be thin and firm, tightly fastened to the sides, and removed once baby is able to pull herself up to stand.

Other Suggestions

- Place baby's crib near your bed for close contact and to make nighttime feedings a bit more convenient. The AAP recommends keeping your baby's crib in your room for the first year of life to help reduce the risk of SIDS.
- Alternate which side of baby's head is on the mattress each week to avoid positional plagiocephaly (flat spots on the head). Turn her head to one side one week when you put her down to sleep, and turn it to the other side the following week.
- While she's awake, give baby plenty of tummy time (lying on her tummy) every day to help her strengthen her back muscles and enhance her motor development.
- Offer baby a pacifier for sleeping (naps and nighttime); pacifiers have been found to reduce the risk of SIDS. (For breastfeeding babies, wait about a month before introducing a pacifier so breastfeeding is well established first.) You don't

need to replace the pacifier if it comes out of her mouth while sleeping; the benefit appears to be related to starting the sleep cycle with a pacifier, not continuing all night long. (For more on pacifiers, see Chapter Eleven.)

Part Two

Growth, Development, and Practical Life Skills

We have organized your baby's growth and development during the first year of life around the ages at which your child will be going to scheduled visits to see her doctor. Not only does this pattern provide a chronological course of development for the first year, it also helps you prepare for your scheduled visits with the doctor.

Chapters Five through Ten cover a variety of topics, including expected growth and development as well as practical issues such as feeding your baby, handling sleep issues, and understanding important safety matters. You will find answers to questions that many parents have during their baby's first year, as well as suggested topics that you might want to discuss with your physician.

Although each chapter in this section can stand alone, we encourage you to read them all in order. To avoid repetition, most issues are covered in-depth only once. Some of these matters are explored in greater depth in the third section of this book under Hot Topics. If you have additional questions about a topic, you can look there for more information.

5

Your Baby at Two Weeks

Congratulations! You have survived, possibly even thrived, with your new baby at home. Now it is time to pack him up and take him to his first visits to the doctor's office. The expected well-child visits in the first year occur one to three days after discharge from the hospital, then at two to three weeks of age, then at two, four, six, nine, and twelve months of age. Remember to allow extra time for these trips; it is amazing how much time it takes to get a newborn ready to travel in the car, especially if he spits up or needs a diaper change right after you get him dressed. Also, remember to dress your baby appropriately for the weather, strap him in snugly in the car seat, and don't forget the diaper bag!

Major Topics of the First Two Weeks

The major topics of a well-child visit to the doctor in the first two weeks usually involve the baby's weight and jaundice. As discussed in Chapter Three, all babies will lose weight and may become jaundiced in the first several days of life. The circumstances vary based on the child, but on average, both the maximum amount of weight loss and the highest level of bilirubin (the chemical that causes jaundice) occur on the fourth day of life. That is why the first doctor's visit is scheduled for when your baby is three to five days old.

Baby's Weight

At all well visits, the first order of business is to obtain the baby's weight. Be ready to undress your child completely. For the first several months, most offices like to weigh the baby naked because the extra weight of a diaper or a onesie is significant on a newborn. You can put the diaper back on after the weighing, but it makes the exam easier for the doctor to leave the rest of the clothes off for now. As you might be waiting in the exam room for a while, wrap baby up in a blanket to keep him warm.

You might want to bring a cloth of some sort to put over baby once you've taken off his diaper and are transferring him to the scale—just in case he pees on the way. Either that, or pack an extra shirt for you in the diaper bag!

While most babies lose only 6 to 8 percent of their birth weight, some babies lose more than 10 percent and become significantly dehydrated. This is an issue of particular concern for breastfeeding moms. It may be that mom's milk is not completely in yet and thus baby is not getting a full amount of breast milk. It may be that your baby is small or slightly premature and tires easily while eating or breastfeeding. For whatever reason, some babies are not able to eat for long enough periods of time to gain weight. If a baby has lost too much weight by this visit, he will need to be more closely monitored and if you are breastfeeding, you would probably benefit from contacting a lactation consultant for help. (See Chapter Eleven on breastfeeding for more details.) The doctor will schedule him for regular weight checks until it is clear that he is gaining an appropriate amount of weight. On average, a baby will gain one ounce per day, but the range for healthy babies is one-half ounce to two ounces per day.

Keeping a Diaper Diary

It is helpful to keep a record of your baby's wet diapers and bowel movements for the first few days after you leave the hospital. By day three, his stools should have changed from the dark green color they were at birth to the transitional green/yellow stools, and turned into the seedy mustard yellow stools of a normal newborn. As for wet diapers, a simple rule of thumb is that a baby should have the same number of wet diapers as the number of days he is old plus one more. So a three-day-old baby should have four (three plus one) wet diapers in twenty-four hours. This will level off at around eight to ten wet diapers a day.

Jaundice

Most babies are checked before they leave the hospital to see if their bilirubin level is too high. However, as mentioned, jaundice usually continues to get worse, with an average peak around the fourth day of life. If your baby looks more yellow than expected when seen by your physician, the bilirubin might need to be checked again. Remember, the danger level for bilirubin depends on how many days old, how premature, and how sick the baby is.

There are several ways to check the bilirubin level. The first is just by seeing how

What You Can Do
Bilirubin is processed by the liver and excreted through baby's pee and poop. To help prevent or lessen the jaundice, you need to feed your baby often (at least every two to three hours) during the first weeks of life to help him move the excess bilirubin out of his system.

yellow the baby is. (For babies with medium and darker skin tones, this visual checking is not as effective and transcutaneous bilirubin or blood tests are more accurate.) In general, jaundice starts in the face and moves down the chest and abdomen and then down the legs. If jaundice has spread to the lower abdomen but not the legs, this usually corresponds to a roughly estimated bilirubin level of 15 (a safe level—see below for the interpretation of bilirubin levels).

In order to measure the bilirubin level most accurately, blood needs to be drawn from your baby. However, in the last few years, an alternative but less accurate measurement called transcutaneous bilirubin has become common. This method is painless because it only involves laying a probe on your baby's forehead for several seconds to "measure" the color of the skin. In addition, this method is faster, with results in under a minute. The blood test results take about an hour.

The slight drawback of transcutaneous bilirubin is that it is not as accurate as the blood measurement—the results vary by 2 to 3 points. Thus if the danger level is 19 and the transcutaneous bilirubin is 15.5, you can safely skip the blood test because 15.5 plus 3 points is still below the danger level of 19. However, if the transcutaneous bilirubin is 19.5, the actual blood level might be anywhere from 16.5 to 22.5. In this case, the doctor would do the blood test to find the actual bilirubin level and see if any action is necessary.

If the blood bilirubin level is above the danger level your baby will need some intervention, usually phototherapy. This used to require hospitalization for one to two days, but recently outpatient phototherapy, also known as a "bili blanket," has become more available. A bili blanket has stiff plastic tubes running through it that emit the special blue light that treats jaundice. Your baby can be wrapped up in the blanket and get the required phototherapy at home. This often involves a lot of logistics to get the blanket and arrange for follow-up measurements of the bilirubin to make sure the phototherapy is working. For some families, it is worth the effort to avoid having to stay in the hospital.

Once the bilirubin level is below the danger zone and heading down, you almost never have to worry about jaundice again. The body takes over processing the bilirubin, and the yellow color will resolve itself slowly over the next one to three weeks. So if your physician says, by any measurement, that the jaundice is not significant, you have passed that milestone safely.

Common Questions in the First Few Weeks

Why does my baby have crusty or goopy eyes?

Babies are born with small, easily collapsible tear ducts that connect the eye and nose. Normally when you cry, these tear ducts drain the fluid from your eye to the nose. If this duct is clogged or closed, though, material backs up, creating a discharge from the eye. In addition, material builds up because babies can't wipe their eyes like older children or adults.

The simple treatment for clogged tear ducts is to gently wipe the eyes with a warm, wet washcloth. This will loosen and remove the material. If the problem persists, massaging the duct, which is found between the lower inner corner of the eye and the nose, can be helpful.

You should know that this problem can persist for months, coming and going at different times. It can also switch eyes, affecting one eye at one time and the other eye a few weeks later, or both at once. If these symptoms persist beyond a year, there is a minor surgery available to open the ducts, but that is rarely needed.

When can we start to use a pacifier?

Pacifiers are a wonderful way of soothing your baby. As parents around the world have noted, sucking is a very soothing process for infants. However, pacifiers occasionally can cause nipple confusion and interfere with breastfeeding. Our suggestion is that if you are breastfeeding, hold off on pacifiers until nursing is well established and your baby is gaining weight in a healthy pattern. This usually occurs around two weeks of age. If you are exclusively bottle feeding, then there is no issue with nipple confusion, and you can start pacifiers immediately.

Pros and Cons of Pacifiers

Pros

- Sucking on a pacifier is soothing and can calm your baby.
- It satisfies a baby's need to suck.
- You don't need mom's breast or dad's finger for the baby to calm down (which can be a real blessing when you're driving somewhere).
- It helps baby relax and fall asleep.
- Research suggests that using a pacifier when falling asleep decreases the risk of SIDS.

Cons

- Babies can get nipple confusion, which results in baby not latching onto the breast correctly anymore and therefore causing mom pain. (This is less of an issue if breastfeeding is well established and the pacifier is not started until the baby is a month old.)
- Some babies need the pacifier to sleep and thus cry when it falls out of their mouth at night. It can be very tiring to get up to replace it or try to find it in the dark.
- Babies who use pacifiers tend to stop breastfeeding earlier than babies who never used a pacifier.
- Pacifiers may increase the risk of middle ear infections.

Note: If you decide to use a pacifier, never attach it to your baby with a string long enough to go around the baby's neck because this could choke him. And buy extras; they are easily lost.

When can I take my baby out in public, and where can we go?

The simple answer is that your baby can go wherever you go, whether it is a holiday party, the grocery store, or a baseball game. The real concern is about what illnesses the baby might catch going out in public. You can help protect your baby by keeping him close to you, either in your arms or in a sling. If other people have to go through you to look at or hold your baby, you have more control over who gets close to him. The second line of defense is hand washing. *Everyone* must wash their hands before they touch the baby. Keeping a portable hand sanitizer in your stroller or diaper bag is helpful for when you are out. Finally, be sure to stand at least three feet away from anyone with a cold, cough, or the sniffles, as this is the distance a sneeze will send droplets.

By the way, when babies sneeze, it does not necessarily mean they are sick. They regularly sneeze in the first few weeks of life when their nose is tickled. But isn't it cute?

Growth and Development in the First Few Weeks

Your baby is a marvelous creation full of potential. However, in the first few weeks of life, he can only control a few of his muscles. Most of his motion is random. For example, there are six muscles in each eye. At first, the muscles are uncoordinated and the eyes are often crossed, looking in different directions. It takes a few weeks before he can control them well enough to consistently hold a steady gaze. By four months, his eye control will be good enough to follow objects around the room.

This does not mean that a fixed gaze cannot happen at birth. Studies have clearly shown that at certain times babies can mimic adult facial movements. It is fun to try this at home. Choose an alert quiet time, when your baby is neither sleepy nor crying, but just peacefully looking around at the world. Lay him down, either flat on his back or on his side to help him keep his head stable.

Then slowly change your facial expression, opening your mouth or raising your eyebrows over a few seconds. If you are lucky, a few seconds later you will see your baby make the same face. For fascinating information about infant skills in the first few days of life, we highly recommend you check out *Your Amazing Newborn* by Marshall and Phyllis Klaus.

For many parents it is helpful to think about the first year of motor development as progressing from head to toe. At first your newborn's head wobbles and wiggles and only rarely stays up straight. However, by two months, he will hold his head up straight more often, with limited wobbling, and by four months it will be very stable. Similarly your baby's hand control will progress over four months. He will start with random waving, poking himself in the eyes and scratching his face at birth. At around two to three months of age, he will stop hitting himself and start hitting objects dangling in front of him. Finally, at around four months he will begin grasping objects and bringing them to his mouth to explore.

At around four to six months, your baby will start controlling the torso muscles that are needed for sitting up. Next will come control over his legs for crawling at around six to nine months, and then walking at around twelve months. This head-to-toe pattern makes it easy for you to anticipate the progression of motor development during the first year.

Safety in the First Few Weeks

Smoking

The most important safety issue is smoking. Everyone knows that smoking is unhealthy for the entire household. Even if parents smoke outside, their children are still exposed to some smoke (on the parent's skin, clothes, and breath) and have more ear infections and illnesses, and experience more wheezing. Smoking is also associated with a higher risk of household burns and fires. It also increases the risk of SIDS. If someone in your household is still smoking, now is the time to stop.

A related safety issue is verifying that all of your household smoke detectors work. It is a good idea to check the batteries monthly and change them regularly—every six months is a good rule of thumb. Also, make sure you have enough smoke detectors and consider a mix of hard-wired and battery-operated detectors, so you have backup in case the power goes out. Check the expiration date on your smoke detectors because some detectors have a limited life and need to be replaced every ten years. Finally, if you have a wood stove or fireplace, you need a carbon monoxide detector if you don't have one already.

Car Seat

A car seat is one of the most important tools you have for protecting your baby from harm. In the United States and Canada, child passenger safety laws require car seats for infants. Unfortunately, according to the National Highway Traffic Safety Administration, more than 80 percent of car seats are not installed correctly. So what can you do to improve your odds?

First, remember that babies must face backward in the car seat for the full first year of life—regardless of their weight or height. Next, try to install the car seat in the center position of the rear seat. Studies have shown that to be the safest location for any passenger in a car accident. Also remember that you should never install a rear-facing infant car seat in a front seat that has a passenger-side air bag because it places children at risk of serious injury or death should the air bag deploy during an accident, even at low speeds.

When actually installing the car seat, review the owner's manual and the car seat installation instructions to make sure you understand the mechanics of how it all works. If your car comes equipped with a LATCH system (Lower Anchors and Tethers for Children), use it; studies have shown that it provides additional protection. The LATCH system is a special system of anchors and tethers that firmly locks the car seat into the car. It uses anchors beyond the seat of the car, maybe even in the floor or wall of the car, which provide more support and stability for the car seat. If you have an older vehicle and the seat belts won't lock in position, you will need to use a metal buckle to fix the belts in place (like on an airplane). Finally, pull everything as tight as possible; you may even try pressing your body weight onto the seat by kneeling on it if necessary. If the seat moves more than an inch, readjust the straps until the seat is tighter.

Next you need to adjust the seat for your child. The harnesses should be flat, not twisted. The chest clip should be below the collar bones but above the abdomen—aim for the middle of the sternum (or breast bone), which is in the middle of baby's chest. And the straps should be tight. Most parents are too hesitant in this area and leave the straps too loose. You should be able to slide just one finger between the strap and your baby, but no more.

Finally, get your installation checked by an expert. Look around for car seat events where you can have your car seat checked out. Sometimes local police or fire departments will inspect the car seat for free and even do adjustments for you. And if your community is offering a car seat workshop, sign up for it. It will not only make your child safer, but will also give you the peace of mind that comes with knowing you have installed the seat correctly. If you have access to the Internet, check out the National Highway Traffic Safety Administration website, which maintains a list of car seat inspection stations by zip code. http://www.nhtsa.dot.gov/CPS/CPSFitting/Index.cfm.

Recurring Issues in the First Few Weeks

Sleep

Sleep is a hot topic for all parents. At this stage in life babies will sleep for twelve to sixteen hours a day, sometimes more.

Unfortunately for parents, their sleep is erratic and rarely lasts more than three or four hours in a row. This means that the parents need to learn to sleep when the baby sleeps, which might mean taking daily naps at 11 a.m. Babies also might have day/night reversal, where they sleep soundly during the day but are alert and awake at night. This will pass after a few weeks, but if you want to make it go away faster, you can encourage nighttime sleeping with a dark, quiet, boring room and encourage daytime alertness with light, noise, and stimulating activities. (For more help with sleep issues, see Chapter Fourteen.)

A general rule in child care is never to wake a sleeping baby. This is true except in the first few weeks of life. Babies need to eat frequently to prevent dehydration, avoid jaundice, and gain weight. Regularly nursing babies also helps breastfeeding moms develop an appropriate milk supply. So, for the first few weeks, we recommend that you let your baby sleep no more than four to four and one-half hours in a row. Once the baby is gaining weight and nursing well, usually at around two weeks of age, then it is best to allow your baby to sleep as long as he wants.

New topics in the First Few Weeks

Vitamin D

Another issue in the first year of life is vitamin D supplementation. In general, people get vitamin D from sunlight, when ultraviolet light converts a precursor molecule in the skin to a useable form of vitamin D. However, as more and more people use sunscreen for protection against the dangers of sun exposure, many of them are not getting enough sun exposure to replenish their needed vitamin D. In addition, during the winter there is not only less sun exposure in general but the angle of the sun is such that it cannot convert the precursor molecule to usable vitamin D. Depending on how far away from the equator you live, you might have more than four months of the year when the sun is unable to provide you with needed vitamin D.

The American Academy of Pediatrics recommends a daily supplement of 200 International Units of vitamin D for all infants who are exclusively breastfeeding or who receive less than sixteen ounces of vitamin D fortified formula a day. Fortunately, this amount of vitamin D is easy to obtain from over-the-counter vitamin drops available at your grocery store. Just buy the vitamins in liquid form and put the appropriate amount of drops in your baby's mouth once a day.

Vaccines in the First Few Weeks

In Jamie's office, vaccines are the major topic of conversation at the two- to three-week visit. There are no scheduled shots at this visit, which allows for a leisurely discussion without the pressure of needing to make an immediate decision. (The first set of recommended childhood vaccines doesn't occur until the two-month well-child visit.) Going over the topic in advance with your doctor will give you the opportunity to research your questions before the next well visit. Then when you arrive at the two-month visit, you will be ready with a decision or any questions. In this book, the topic of vaccinations is well covered in Chapter Thirteen.

Even though no vaccines are recommended for your baby at this time, family members and other people with regular exposure to your child are recommended to be vaccinated against pertussis (whooping cough) and influenza. Because babies are not fully immunized against these illnesses until after six months of age, there is some risk that these infections will be transmitted to the infants by older children and adults.

The booster for pertussis in teenagers and adults comes in a vaccine called Tdap. Tdap provides a standard tetanus and diphtheria booster plus an added booster for pertussis. It is recommended for anyone over age ten who has not received a tetanus booster in the last two years. It is especially recommended for women who have just delivered a baby, and many hospitals now offer it before discharge.

The influenza vaccine is recommended for all regular contacts of infants under six months of age during the flu season. This includes the mother, who might have received that vaccine during pregnancy, as well as other adults and children in the household. It also means other childcare providers. If relatives regularly watch your baby during the flu season, you should ask if they have received a flu shot. If not, you might offer to pay for them to get it; the cost is around twenty-five dollars.

Your Baby at Two Months

The two-month birthday comes at a point of transition in your baby's first year. The adrenaline rush of birth and having your beautiful baby in your arms gives way to the daily routines of eating, sleeping, and changing diapers. Sleep deprivation sets in. The first year is like a marathon, and takes patience and perseverance to finish gracefully. So remember our earlier advice to pace yourself, take care of yourself, and accept help from others. (Practice saying this phrase over and over: "Yes, that would be lovely.")

Major Topics at Two Months

The major topic at your baby's two-month birthday is sleep. By now most children have settled into routines and will be getting twelve to sixteen hours of sleep a day. Day/night reversal has faded and your baby should be sleeping more at night than during the day. Three solid naps during the day are common, with an occasional cat nap in between. Nighttime sleeping is the major issue for parents at this time, as they wonder if their child will ever sleep through the night.

A Word on "Sleeping through the Night"

From the medical perspective, "sleeping through the night" is defined as sleeping five hours in a row. So expecting a baby to sleep for eight to ten hours in a row is as unrealistic as it is unlikely. It can happen, but this is incredibly rare, despite what you may hear anecdotally.

Waking up in the middle of the night is common and expected of your baby. Most of the time, a simple feeding will suffice to help your baby fall back to sleep. Occasionally, something more is needed, such as rocking or walking your baby. That might be okay with you—some parents love connecting with their baby in a rocking chair in the middle of the night. It is a quiet time to bond with your baby without the distraction of household chores or other children. However, if your baby is rocked back to sleep every night, then she will learn to expect it—now and for the next several months. That might become tiring and harder on you and your family as you become more sleep-deprived.

Start setting up good sleep habits now. First, recognize that not all nighttime noises require intervention. Some baby squeaks and fusses are transient, and she may not be actually waking up when she makes noises like these during the night. Wait and listen before picking her up, just in case what you're hearing are natural sleeping noises. If she does wake up and is hungry, you might want to try letting her eat to the point of drowsiness, then put her down to fall asleep on her own. If she does not settle and begins to get upset, pick her up and try again. Let her get drowsy, almost asleep, and lay her down. Also avoid changing diapers in the middle of the night unless they are poopy or have leaked. A baby is more likely to fully wake up with the stimulation of a diaper change, which means it will be harder to get her back to sleep. Finally, white noise, such as a fan, the radio playing quietly between stations, or even a vacuum cleaner, is a wonderful tool to help babies fall asleep.

For more information on sleep issues, see Chapter Fourteen.

Common Questions at Two Months

Should I be concerned that my baby only has a bowel movement every two or three days?

Babies can poop seven times a day or once every seven days, and both extremes can both be normal. What matters is how the baby is acting. If a baby only poops once every three to four days and isn't uncomfortable, then all is fine. However, many parents report that by day three or four, they notice some fussiness in their baby that disappears after a bowel movement. If that is the case, then you might want to try some tricks to encourage a bowel movement on day two. These tricks might include abdominal massage, gently bicycling baby's legs, and, occasionally, rectal stimulation with a thermometer. (Lubricate the thermometer with petroleum jelly and don't insert it more than one inch into the rectum).

While we are on the topic, parents often ask about diarrhea and constipation at this visit. Normal newborn stools are thin, yellow, somewhat watery, and full of seedy material. Diarrhea is stool so watery that it has no shape and is pure liquid, so seven stools a day (if it has some form to it) is not diarrhea. It is just a normal variation. A stool every seven days is not constipation; constipation is hard, firm stool. If your baby seems to be straining to poop but the stool comes out soft or mushy, that is not constipation. She is just straining to poop while lying down. It's not easy to poop while flat on your back.

My baby's breathing is really noisy. Should I be worried?

The simple answer is that this is a factor of small airways. The narrower the airway, the more resistance it generates as air passes through it. Increased resistance leads to more noise with breathing. This noise becomes exaggerated with anything that narrows the airway even more, such as mucus from a cold, which is why you will often find babies breathing even louder when they are sick. (Jamie calls that Darth Vader breathing.) It is scary but not dangerous.

So, what kind is dangerous? Fast and labored breathing. If a baby is breathing fast—more than sixty breaths a minute—that is cause for concern. (You have to count the number of breaths for a full minute to get an accurate count, because babies normally have very irregular breathing from moment to moment.) The other important factor to examine is how much effort your baby is using to breathe. Imagine runners at the end of a long race. They will be breathing hard, raising their shoulders to open their airways, and you might see their skin suck in between their ribs. If you see those same signs in your baby, she is having significant respiratory distress and you need to call your doctor immediately. (See Chapter Sixteen for more information on breathing problems.)

Why does my baby's head look flat?
Ever since physicians have recommended that babies sleep on their backs to prevent SIDS, more parents have noticed that their baby's head is flatter in back. This condition, formally called plagiocephaly, usually occurs due to external pressure on the back of the skull. To treat it, alternate which side of the head the baby sleeps on and avoid putting your baby on her back when she's awake. This means that you should encourage tummy time and upright cuddle time more than time spent lying on her back, tucked into a car seat, or in other reclining sitting positions. If the plagiocephaly persists or is not noticed until later in life, there are more controversial treatments such as molding helmets that you can discuss with your doctor.

Growth Curves at Two Months

One of the most common questions from every parent is, "How is my baby growing?" At every well visit, the doctor will measure your baby's weight and length, as well as head circumference, and plot them out on growth curves. These curves allow you to see your baby's growth over time as well as to compare her size and growth to other children her age.

The first thing to understand about these curves is that they don't say how healthy your child is. A child in the 10th percentile for weight can be just as healthy as a child in the 95th percentile. The actual value is less important than the overall growth trend. A child whose weight was in the 50th percentile a month ago, but is now in the 95th percentile, might be on the way to becoming obese. A child who is dropping percentiles might have an illness that is preventing her from gaining weight, or she might just be genetically predestined to be petite. All of this information needs to be evaluated by your doctor in context.

The next point is that curves may not be pertinent to your child. Special populations of children, such as those with Down syndrome, have special growth curves. Premature babies (preemies) also have their own curves. However, while most preemies will attain the normal growth curves over a matter of months, children with Down syndrome will always have their own growth curves.

Another issue with growth curves is that the measurements can be inaccurate. While weighing a child on a scale is consistent and reproducible, measuring a baby's length and head circumference is very operator-dependent. The wiggle factor in little babies can be huge. It doesn't help that a half-inch in head circumference might change a baby from 95 percent to 50 percent. So remember to take the length and head circumference measurements with a grain of salt.

It is fun to see how your baby is progressing along her growth curves. Offices with electronic medical records should be able to print out a copy with a touch of the button. Ask your doctor's office if they can print out your baby's growth curve when you are at each well-child visit.

Growth and Development at Two Months

The first two months of life are full of wonderful skill development. Over this time, your baby will learn how to hold up her head. It will still wobble at times, but she'll be able to hold it steady for short periods of time. In addition, her eyes will track and follow you, not perfectly, but for short distances. She will also be startled by loud noises such as a dog barking or a phone ringing, and should be beginning to grasp toys, such as rattles. But the most fun activity will be her smiling. Somewhere in the first two months she should have learned how to focus on your face and smile at you—and that smile will light you up from the inside out!

Language development also begins at around two months. Babies will babble and coo at this age and will respond to your voice. This is the perfect time to start reading books to your baby, if you haven't already started. Not only will it expose her to words and the rhythms of language but it will also provide some close bonding time for the two of you. Rhyming books are usually best at this age, as are books with high-contrast illustrations. Some early infant books have only black-and-white pictures to enhance the contrast. Babies also love to look at photographs of other babies and young children.

The next two months will show even more motor skill development. With her increased head and neck strength, and her improved control over her eye muscles, she will be able to follow you with her eyes 180 degrees around the room. Her hands will also become more dexterous, and she'll no longer hit herself in the face but will hit things in front of her instead. This is a great opportunity to place hanging toys within reach. She will learn to control her arms and hands by batting at them. Your baby will also learn to grasp toys and bring them to her mouth.

One skill she might also develop in the next two months is rolling over. While most babies don't roll over until after four months of age, some babies do it sooner. If a baby is able to roll over, then they are also able to roll off of things, like a changing table. For safety's sake, keep an even closer eye on your baby when she's on the changing table to prevent her from rolling off.

Safety at Two Months

The safety concerns at two months of age have not changed significantly from when your baby was a newborn. Stop smoking if you are currently smoking; make sure the smoke detectors, carbon monoxide detectors, and fire extinguishers are in proper working order; and make sure the car seat fits safely in the car. Also, be sure to check the hot water temperature in your home. Babies can be scalded if they accidentally come into contact with water over 170 degrees Fahrenheit, which is possible if your hot water heater is set too high. The recommended temperature of your water is 120 degrees. A simple way to check the temperature is to run the water until it is as hot as possible, and then try to hold your hand under it for ten seconds. If the water is too hot to do that, then it would be much too hot for your baby.

> You should continue vitamin D supplements for your baby if you are nursing exclusively, or if you are both nursing and bottle feeding and your baby is taking less than sixteen ounces of formula a day.

One final note: Over the next two months your baby will develop the ability to grab an object and bring it to her mouth to taste and explore it orally. While she is not particularly mobile at this point, she still might be able to reach for small objects such as earrings or a pin next to the diaper changing table. If she grabs such an object and accidentally swallows it, she could choke. Now is a good time to start childproofing your house.

Postpartum Depression

The two-month milestone is also a common time for postpartum depression to set in—for both mom *and* dad. Dads, just like moms, are vulnerable to a roller coaster of emotions in their baby's first year. It is common to have spells of tears or to feel blue at times. What is not common is to have a persistent feeling of being overwhelmed or of having a black cloud hanging over every activity of the day. Parents with depression do function. They can take care of their children, but they feel no joy in doing so. They are irritable, cranky, and unhappy, and would prefer to just roll over in bed and pull the covers over their heads.

If you find yourself feeling this way, talk to your doctor or midwife about it. Recognize, however, that you may not be able to see your depression in yourself and that you might have to listen to your family and friends when they tell you that you need help. And don't be afraid of being labeled "crazy." Depression is an illness and nothing to be ashamed of. Your mood may even be related to an undetected medical problem such as a thyroid disorder. Many women have problems with an over- or under-active thyroid in the months after pregnancy. You may need therapy or medication to help you regain your mood. But don't just live with these feelings—do something to regain the joy you felt over the birth of your new baby.

Vaccines at Two Months

The two-month well visit marks the beginning of the recommended routine vaccine schedule, which includes eight recommended vaccines. These same eight vaccines are repeated at the four- and six-month well visits. The recommended vaccines are:

- Haemophilus influenza type B (HIB)
- Pneumococcal vaccine
- Diphtheria, tetanus, and acellular pertussis (DTaP)
- Hepatitis B
- Inactivated polio (IPV) and
- Rotavirus

Of these, rotavirus is an oral vaccine and hepatitis B, DTaP, and IPV can be combined into one needle. This means your baby only needs three injections and one vaccine by mouth. Full details on these and all vaccines given in the first year of life can be found in Chapter Thirteen.

With all vaccines comes the potential for side effects. Most babies will cry when they receive their shots but then calm down quickly. They may fall asleep on the way home. Some babies are fine right away, while many others are still cranky and out of sorts for a day or two. A minority of babies will develop a fever and a small number will develop a high fever, over 102 degrees Fahrenheit. They might also develop soreness or redness at the site of the injection and a few children will have a lump in their leg for several days after the vaccination. These are the common and minor side effects. If your baby has these symptoms and she is relieved with pain medications, cool compresses, comforting, and time, then there's no need to call your doctor. (See page 86 at the end of this chapter for more information about pain medications for your baby.)

Unfortunately, in rare cases a baby's reaction to vaccination is more serious. If you notice more severe side effects such as nonstop crying for more than three hours or a seizure, you should *immediately* call your doctor—don't delay. Your baby will probably need to be seen that day and might need to go to the emergency room for an evaluation. You can obtain a list of the more serious side effects on the Vaccine Information Sheets (VIS) that your doctor is required to give you every time your child gets a vaccine. You can also research the side effects of vaccines online or in vaccine information books.

Remember that while we do encourage you to follow the recommended schedule, you can create your own schedule, spreading the vaccines out and delaying some if you want. Please also remember that people who are in regular contact with your baby (that's mom, dad, siblings, grandparents, or anyone who lives with the baby or spends time with her on a daily or weekly basis) are recommended to receive the influenza vaccine during flu season and a *pertussis* (whooping cough) booster vaccine at any time of year.

There are two common, over-the-counter medicines for pain that you can safely give your baby: acetaminophen (brand name: Tylenol) and ibuprofen (brand name: Advil, Motrin, and others). Both of these medications come in several strengths, including infant drops and children's suspension. *Be extra careful when figuring the dosage.* Please make sure that you are using the correct dosing sheet for the type of liquid medicine you have at home. Do not make the mistake of using the dosing sheet for the children's suspension to calculate how much volume of liquid of the infant drops to give to your baby. The infant drops are much more concentrated, so giving a higher volume of drops can lead to an overdose. If you are not certain how much to give, ask your baby's doctor.

In general, ibuprofen lasts longer, around six hours at a time, and does a better job of bringing down a high fever. However, ibuprofen can upset a baby's stomach so we don't recommend using it if the baby is vomiting or has diarrhea. Acetaminophen only lasts four hours at a time but is easier on the stomach.

7

Your Baby at Four Months

The four-month milestone is a bit of a breather because you've done it all before. There are no new vaccines; the safety, growth, and development issues have not changed much; and you and your baby should have settled into a routine by now, with regular patterns for eating, sleeping, and other activities. By now, most parents will have found their groove and have learned to pace themselves for the long haul.

Major Topics at Four Months

Perhaps the issue Jamie stresses most at the four-month well-child visit is how well mom and dad are taking care of *themselves*. Your baby's first year will probably be one of the most stressful years of your life. You have gone from being an adult with a main responsibility of taking care of yourself to being a parent, responsible for the life and wellbeing of another—one of the biggest transitions you will ever face. The life that was once focused on yourself and your spouse or partner is now focused on this small, dependent little miracle. Your priorities, your friends, and your daily activities will have changed radically.

Some people welcome these changes with joy. They radiate happiness, and find great fulfillment in caring for a baby. Others experience resentment and a feeling of loss as a result of these changes. Maybe they were not ready to be parents. Maybe they miss going out for drinks after work with friends or to the movies with their spouse. Maybe they miss sleeping in on a Saturday morning or reading a book in peace.

Most of us fall somewhere in the middle. We treasure the joys found and grieve the opportunities lost. We recognize this as a milestone in life, then learn new skills and find our hidden talents. In our more mature moments, we appreciate how we are growing into our new roles as parents.

Whatever your response, it helps to acknowledge your feelings. Understand that they are normal. It is normal to be over the moon and talking about the baby to family and friends every chance you get. It is normal to be frustrated when he spits up all over his new outfit seconds before you leave the house. It is normal to be sad that you can't go visit a friend for a weekend because your baby is sick with a temperature of 103. It is normal to have all these feelings in the same day, or maybe even the same hour.

Stress is hard on your body, so as we have said many times before, remember to take care of yourself. Sleep as much as you can. (Make this your mantra: "Sleep when the baby sleeps.") Exercise with or without the baby—many gyms have daycare available for members—or go for walks with your baby in the backpack or stroller. Remember to accept help when offered. (Don't forget to say: "Yes, that would be lovely.")

Another concrete step to staying healthy is taking breaks. Even a fifteen-minute shower or quiet walk around the block can recharge your batteries. And a forty-five-minute nap might just be heavenly! So ask your family for some coverage. Find other parents to share care. Babysitting swaps not only provide respite, but they also allow you to share your joys and concerns with other adults at the same stage of life.

Most of all, have fun! Your baby will only be this little once.

Common Questions at Four Months

Can I start feeding baby solid foods now?

The national and international recommendations are to exclusively breastfeed your baby for six months, and we strongly support this. However, we recognize that many parents in the United States start supplementary foods before six months of age. Keep in mind that you are actually not introducing foods for their nutritional well-being during the first year, but for developing baby's palate, so there's no reason to rush into it. If you feel that you must start solids before the six-month well-child visit, please read more about starting foods in Chapters Eight and Fifteen.

My baby is drooling so much and chewing on everything. Do you think he is teething?

When babies are teething, you will find them drooling a lot and chewing on anything they can put in their mouths. But this is also the general behavior of most babies around four months old, even if they aren't teething. So while some babies are actually teething at four months, many babies don't develop teeth until after they are six months old. The drooling and mouthing you see is a normal developmental stage that babies go through at this age.

The way to tell if your baby is getting a tooth is to feel his gums; the obvious proof of teething is a tooth. When a tooth cuts through the gum, it hurts, so be prepared to comfort your baby. Cold objects to chew on are helpful, so put some favorite chewable toys in the refrigerator. You can also find some teething rings that are designed to go into the freezer. There are over-the-counter topical medicines like benzocaine that will numb the gum when spread over the area where the tooth is coming through. Finally, if the discomfort seems extreme you can try oral pain medicines like acetaminophen or ibuprofen, which usually last longer than the topical benzocaine.

My baby is getting rashes. Should I be concerned?

Many babies develop rashes at around four months. Some rashes on the face are directly related to a baby's drooling and the saliva that is wiped away from his cheeks and chin, which get dry and raw. Fortunately these rashes will go away as the child gets older and drools less. Another common rash is *atopic dermatitis* or eczema. This is a more widespread rash with dry, red skin that concentrates on the face, elbows, and knees, but might extend out to the rest of the body. Eczema is worse in the winter, better in the summer, and can usually be managed with copious amounts of lotions and occasionally a mild, over-the-counter 1% hydrocortisone cream. See your doctor if the rash doesn't go away with the simple treatments or if the skin is cracked or bleeding.

Rashes are also associated with certain illnesses. Viral rashes are less likely to include dry skin as a symptom and are more likely to be flat dots over various parts of the body. It is virtually impossible to diagnose a rash over the phone so if you have any concerns, you need to take your baby to a doctor to make sure the rash is benign.

Is it okay to put my child in an upright harness at this age?

Once your baby has enough muscular control to ensure that his head won't flop around without your support, you can put him in a safe upright harness. Examples include backpacks, a stationary activity center (commonly known as an exersaucer), or a bouncing harness that hangs from a doorframe or stand. With the exception of the backpack, you will probably not use most of these harnesses for more than a couple of months so you might want to borrow them from someone else or look for them at garage sales instead of buying them new.

For safety reasons, don't put your baby in a baby walker. If your baby "walks" to the top of the stairs and a wheel slips over the edge, he can end up toppling down the entire flight of stairs with no way to stop himself. Canada has banned the sale of baby walkers due to the number of significant injuries that many babies have suffered in this way.

Growth and Development at Four Months

At four months of age, your baby will have good but maybe not perfect control of his head and eyes. He should be able to track you as you walk around the room, smoothly coordinating his head, neck, and eyes. There might still be the slightest head bobble, but if there is anything more, or if you are still noticing crossed eyes, bring that up with your doctor at this visit.

Your baby also will have gained some skills with his hands and will be able to grab objects and bring them to his mouth. While he will likely be trying to roll over, only a few babies actually succeed before four months of age so don't worry if he hasn't accomplished that skill yet. Language-wise, he should still be babbling and cooing, and of course smiling at you.

The next two months will bring progress on several fronts. Your baby's hands will get even more dexterous, and he will learn to use both hands in combination when grabbing objects and putting them in his mouth. Some babies even learn to transfer objects from one hand to the other before six months of age.

The other big growth area will be torso control. He will learn to roll over, at least to one side and usually to both sides, in the next two months. He may also learn to sit up on his own. Most babies will not be completely stable by six months but will be able to sit upright without toppling over for several seconds at a time.

Your baby will still be growing rapidly; on average, babies double their birth weight by five months of age.

Safety Concerns at Four Months

The safety issues are only slightly different at this age. Stop smoking if you are currently smoking, make sure the smoke detectors and fire extinguishers work, and make sure the car seat fits safely in the car. Check the hot water temperature again and make sure that it is around 120 degrees Fahrenheit. As discussed earlier, avoid baby walkers altogether, or at least keep your baby from using them near stairs.

As your baby learns to roll, he may be able to roll over two or three times in a row, effectively becoming "mobile." Be sure he cannot roll over to the top of a flight of stairs, and never leave him unattended on a raised surface such as a bed or changing table. Finally, watch out for objects within reach that might be a choking hazard for him; everything that he can hold onto will go into his mouth.

As a general rule, if an object can pass through the cardboard tube from a roll of toilet paper, it is too small for your baby to safely handle.

Finally, be careful as your baby starts to sit up by himself. Do not ever leave him unattended while he's sitting up because he will be unsteady for several months and in danger of hurting himself by falling. He especially needs you to protect him from falling backward. If he falls sideways or forward he may catch himself on his arms (though that is a learned behavior), but if he falls backward he will hit his head—hard.

Recurring Issues at Four Months

Sleep will still be a hard issue for most parents. Babies normally wake up at least two times a night to eat at this age, and parents become more sleep deprived. Encourage him to fall asleep on his own by letting him get drowsy while nursing or taking a bottle and then putting him into bed. That way, if he happens to wake up in the middle of the night but is not hungry enough to eat, he will have experience in going to sleep without help or a feeding.

Please remember to continue vitamin D supplements for your baby if you are exclusively breastfeeding or if your baby's formula intake is less than sixteen ounces per day. And also remember to read to your baby for at least twenty minutes a day. Not only will this provide you and your baby quality quiet time together, but it will also help him to develop a larger vocabulary as he grows.

Vaccines at Four Months

At your baby's four-month well visit, he will be given boosters for the eight recommended vaccines given at the two-month well visit. Once again, those vaccines are:
- Haemophilus influenza type B (HIB)
- Pneumococcal vaccine
- Diphtheria, tetanus, and acellular pertussis (DTaP)
- Hepatitis B
- Inactivated polio (IPV) and
- Rotavirus

Of these, rotavirus is an oral vaccine, and hepatitis B, DTaP, and IPV can be combined into one needle, which means your baby only needs three injections and one vaccine by mouth.

If your baby received the birth dose of the hepatitis B vaccine in the hospital, he is not required to receive it at the four-month well visit. However, hepatitis B often is combined with other vaccines, so not getting it at this visit might require giving more injections because the other vaccines will have to be given separately. It is not harmful to receive hepatitis B at this visit, so it is up to you to decide if you prefer that he get an extra dose or an extra needle. Full details on these and all vaccines given in the first year of life can be found in Chapter Thirteen.

Remember that you do not have to follow the recommended schedule. You can request that the vaccines be given using an alternative schedule. Many parents are hesitant to have multiple vaccines given to their child at once and are more accepting of the process if the vaccines are spread out, with maybe one or two vaccines at this visit and the rest one or two weeks later. Discuss your concerns and options with your physician.

If you had any concerns regarding your baby's reaction to the vaccines given at the last well visit, please bring them up with your physician at the beginning of the visit. She might remind you that the reaction falls within the normal spectrum or review with you how to use medications to alleviate pain or fevers. Alternatively, she might suggest changing the pattern of vaccinations to determine which vaccine is associated with which reaction.

Please also remember that people in your household who come in contact with your baby are recommended to receive the influenza vaccine during flu season and a pertussis (whooping cough) booster vaccine at any time of year.

8

Your Baby at Six Months

Jamie's theme at the six-month well-child visit is potential. Your baby is about to develop some amazing skills. She is at the cusp of mobility—sitting, then scooting, then crawling. She will gain fine motor skills such as the ability to feed herself. And she will begin interacting with others—smiling or playing, or possibly pulling away if she develops stranger anxiety. It is awe-inspiring to think of who she will become over the next three months.

Major Topics at Six Months

The major topic at six months is how to start solid foods. Around six months of age, most children are ready to start supplementary foods. There are several clues that your baby is ready for foods other than breast milk or formula. First, she should be truly interested in the food. Babies are always interested in what we are doing and will want to play with the food on our plates, but usually they can be distracted by a toy or a game. At some point however, your baby will be so interested in food that nothing else will distract her.

Second, she should possess certain motor skills before you start feeding her solid food. Her torso control should be relatively good. Even if she cannot sit up by herself, she should be able to lean against the side of her high chair and stay stable, as opposed to sliding down into a heap. In addition, she should have reasonable hand–mouth coordination; she should be able to take the food off the high-chair tray and put it in her mouth by herself.

When starting solid foods, it helps to have a sense of humor, plus access to a bath and laundry. At first, your baby will treat food as a new toy—something to be played with but not necessarily eaten. She will put it in her mouth to see what it feels like and her hands will get messy. Then she will miss her mouth and her face will get messy. Then she will get distracted and run her hands through her hair and that will get messy too. And after than she will play the gravity game, and the food will fall to the floor—repeatedly. Starting solid foods is messy!

Most parents find it best to wait until the whole episode is over before trying to clean up. At that point, simply scooping up your baby for a bath is the easiest way to clean her all at once. In addition, having a bare floor (like wood or linoleum) or a tarp or old bed sheet underneath the high chair makes it easier to clean up the mess. And don't forget the camera. Those pictures of baby eating her first foods are priceless!

At first your baby will not understand that food satisfies her hunger. It will take her a while to realize that in addition to tasting good, this new "toy" makes her feel better when she swallows it. Once she makes that connection, she will start asking for food when she's hungry. This doesn't mean that you should stop nursing your baby or giving her bottles. At this age, solids should be given in addition to, not instead of, breast milk or formula.

If you read articles or books on infant feeding, you will find a variety of attitudes on starting solids. Some books even give rules for which foods should come first and how to introduce them. In our opinion, those sorts of rules are a bit excessive. There are a few important guidelines to keep in mind when starting supplementary foods. First, avoid any food your baby might choke on. This is something you'll be well attuned to by now, but don't forget that even cut-up pieces of meat or solid fruits can present a choking hazard. Mushy foods are best when starting. Second, you need to avoid honey in the first year of life. Honey can contain botulism toxin, though it's very rare. Adults and older children are able to degrade the toxin in the digestive tract so that it doesn't cause any damage, but infants are less able to neutralize it. Thus, to avoid botulism poisoning, experts recommend avoiding honey entirely until after your baby's first year. Finally, it is a good idea to avoid cow's milk in the first year of life. Cow's milk has been associated with decreased iron absorption in children.

Beyond these few rules, we feel that almost anything goes. Common starting foods are baby cereal mixed with breast milk, formula or water; applesauce; mashed bananas; avocados; mashed potatoes; yams; and ground-up vegetables. Some books recommend waiting days or even a week between foods. Our attitude is much more relaxed. Feel free to start one new food each day and see how your baby reacts to it. That doesn't mean feeding her that one food alone by itself on a given day. If your baby has already tried cereal, bananas, and avocado, and you want to try mashed potatoes, just add it to the mix and see how she does.

We also encourage trying a variety of foods and even spices. These first few months of exploring solids provide a wonderful opportunity to broaden your baby's palate. Don't be afraid to try exotic fruits, curried dishes, or hot sauces. What might seem exotic to you is probably just run-of-the-mill food elsewhere in the world, so there's no reason to be afraid to let your baby try it. Children often narrow their diet at age two or three and are reluctant to try new foods. If you have started with a wide variety of food during their first year, even when they begin to narrow their diets, they can still enjoy a broad selection of foods.

After giving your baby a new food, if you notice a mild reaction (such as a rash or irritability), you shouldn't ban the food for life. Try it again a few months later. Often a rash or irritability is due to something other than the new food. Only if the food causes the same reaction twice should you avoid it long-term. If there is a severe reaction, however, such as hives or breathing problems, call your doctor immediately to manage the urgent problem, and then talk to your physician before trying the food a second time. It is possible to have a reaction to a food at one age but no reaction later on in life. Many parents also avoid foods that commonly cause allergies until after their baby's first year. Some examples include nuts (such as peanuts, walnuts, and cashews), dairy products, egg whites, fish and shellfish, soy, and wheat products.

Let us reiterate that you don't *have* to start supplementary foods now, and we recommend that you wait until your baby is showing signs that she's ready. (For more information on feeding your baby solid foods, see Chapter Twelve.)

Kids Can Outgrow Food Allergies

A recent example of outgrowing a food allergy came up in Jamie's practice. He saw a child who was failing to gain weight at nine months of age due to a wheat allergy. He instructed her family to stop giving her any wheat products for several months. Her rashes went away, and she gained weight beautifully. Now, at age two, she is eating limited wheat again with minimal complications.

Common Questions at Six Months

Will my baby's eyes change color?

Usually not at this point. While many babies are born with the eye color that they will have for life, many infants' eyes do change color during the first few months. By six months, however, most children have their permanent eye color.

Should my baby be sleeping through the night by now?

The short answer is no. Most babies are not sleeping through the night at this point in time. Although you may hear about those angel children at playgroups or at the park, they are actually quite rare (think Loch Ness monster or Bigfoot!). In addition, many parents have noticed that their baby is sleeping worse now than she was at four months. This frequently occurs because of a growth spurt between five and six months.

If your baby is experiencing a growth spurt, she's going to be hungry more often, which causes a sudden increase in night wakings. Additionally, many babies don't sleep well when they are working through certain developmental skills, and a number of new skills appear during this time. If your baby is still waking up more than three times a night, review Chapter Fourteen and focus again on doing what you can to encourage her to sleep longer. Do keep in mind, though, that if your baby is going through a growth spurt, teething, or approaching a developmental milestone, you may not be able to reduce her night wakings right now. Your sleep encouragement may not have an effect on her wakings until she is through the current phase, but the difficult period will pass eventually.

Growth and Development at Six Months

At six months, your baby will likely be able to sit with support, grab objects with both hands, and even transfer objects from hand to hand. She will also be able to roll over from side to side, sometimes several times in a row. She will babble and coo, and begin to use intonation in her speech.

Over the next three months, the most important skill she will gain is mobility. With exploration as her motivation, she will learn to crawl (although some children bypass that skill entirely and go straight from scooting to walking). She will start out by getting onto all fours, and then learn to pull herself around in "commando" fashion, using her arms to pull herself along while her stomach is still on the floor. The next step is actually crawling on her hands and knees. She may pull herself up on furniture, or even climb up on a step or a stool.

She will also develop some fine motor skills. Starting with a palmar grasp (holding something with the entire hand and making a fist) at six months of age, she will develop a pincer grasp (using just her fingers) by nine to twelve months. She will become more able to pick up smaller items like peas. Also, your baby's growth will begin to slow at this point in time. Whereas the average baby doubled her birth weight by five months of age, she won't triple it until around one year of age.

And finally, her babbling and cooing will start to sound recognizable. At first, she will only produce nonsense sounds like "ma ma ma" or "ba ba ba." However, if you respond enthusiastically and repeat the sounds back to her—"mama"—then your interest will encourage her to repeat them and try new ones. Over many months, this feedback will develop into the beginnings of language.

Safety Concerns at Six Months

With all these new skills come some significant safety concerns. As she becomes more mobile, your baby will come into contact with many potential hazards. (Jamie's son loved to topple potted plants and eat the dirt that spilled onto the floor.) Childproofing your house to safeguard your baby from a variety of hazards will be critical at this point.

In order to childproof your house, you might want to get down on *your* hands and knees and crawl around the house. You will see the world in a different light. You will find hidden choking hazards such as the lost game piece under the couch and the old food under the kitchen table. You will understand why electrical cords and outlets are so fascinating—they are right at eye-level for a crawling baby. And you will identify many other hazards—like the VCR slot that might catch fingers or the runner hanging off the end of the coffee table. Of course, some you won't discover until your baby innocently and curiously points them out to you!

Another big hazard area is stairs. Some babies are early climbers and will learn to climb up steps before they learn to walk. Going up is actually not that dangerous, but coming down can be. Some parents use gates at both the top and bottom of the stairs to prevent tumbles. Be careful though—gates are only helpful if they are closed after every use. Self-latching gates are more useful than those that require you to stop and latch the gate behind you. Other parents don't use gates but do carpet the stairs to make the inevitable tumbles softer. And all parents should try to teach their children as early as possible how to navigate the stairs safely (going down feet first on their tummies).

Do your best to create a "yes" environment for your baby in your home. Make it so you will rarely have to say "No! Don't touch!" That means removing everything that you do not want baby to get her hands or mouth on, if at all possible. Try to make your house a safe place for your baby to explore unhindered by the word "don't." Put the china and crystal figurines away or on a high shelf. Keep all hazardous substances (cleaners, medicines, alcohol, pest control poisons, etc.) in a high cabinet far out of reach or in a locked cupboard. Put plants up out of reach; hide electrical cords; cover outlets; gate the stairs. Your little scientist needs to explore her environment—it's her natural inclination and an extremely important part of her development. Foster that by giving her a safe place to investigate with as few no's as possible.

Consider letting your baby have her own cupboards in the kitchen. Give her free access to the plastic containers drawer. Let her explore the pots and pans cupboard. Put her cups, bowls, and plates in a place where she can reach them. Ask her to put those items away when you are unloading the dishwasher and to get them out to set the table. She'll love helping you and will truly appreciate free access to safe kitchen items. (She'll probably play with those more than her store-bought toys!) Babyproofing and giving your baby safe household items to explore both contribute to making your home a "yes" environment.

This is a good time to mention poison control centers. They are a wonderful—and at times lifesaving—resource you can call any time you have a concern about an accidental ingestion. You should pick up ready-made poison control stickers at your doctor's office or local health department and post them prominently on your home phones, cell phones, refrigerator, and emergency phone lists—anywhere you might think to look when making a call. You should also save the number in any electronic gadgets you carry with you.

There are a couple of things you need to know about poison control stickers. The first is that even though some of them list the name of the local hospital on the sticker, the number given (1-800-222-1222) is actually a national hotline. If you call this number while on vacation a thousand miles away from home, you will automatically be directed to the poison control center that is closest to where you are at that moment. The second thing is that you can call them about anything your baby ingests. You should obviously call if she gets into Aunt Mary's medicine or the cleaning fluid under the sink, but you can also call if she eats potting soil, bubble bath, or a crayon. And they won't make you feel stupid. They have literally heard everything. (If you have any concern at all, then call. This is a "better safe than sorry" issue for sure.)

Finally, you should be aware that physicians no longer recommend keeping syrup of ipecac at home. Syrup of ipecac induces vomiting and used to be kept at home to have on hand if a child ingested a dangerous substance. However, it was often used unnecessarily, causing more problems than the original ingestion. Even if the poison control center determines that vomiting the ingested material would be a good idea, it is safer to do it in a supervised setting such as the emergency room of the local hospital.

As always, stop smoking if you are currently smoking, make sure the smoke detectors, carbon monoxide detectors, and fire extinguishers work, and make sure the car seat fits safely in the car. Check the hot water temperature again and make sure that it is around 120 degrees Fahrenheit. As discussed in an earlier chapter, avoid using baby walkers near stairs or, better yet, avoid them altogether.

Recurring Issues at Six Months

Please remember to continue to read to your baby daily, even if all she wants to do is eat the books. Just by hearing the rhythms of the words coming from your mouth, she will begin to understand the intonations and vocabulary of language. In addition, continue vitamin D supplements for your baby if you are exclusively breast-feeding or if your baby's formula intake is less than sixteen ounces per day.

Depending on where you live, you might need to consider a new supplement at this time: fluoride. Studies suggest that fluoride strengthens teeth and leads to fewer cavities. Although most municipalities fluoridate their water, some don't, and many families are dependent on well water that generally lacks fluoride. It is recommended that children from six to thirty-five months of age who do not have any fluoride in their water should receive a supplement of 0.25 mg of fluoride daily. This usually comes in the form of drops and can easily be mixed with the vitamin D supplements. (There is some controversy over fluoride, so we recommend that you research this issue further. Talk to your dentist and doctor about it. A search on the Internet will give you a good start as well.)

New Topics at Six Months

Stranger Anxiety

Somewhere around four to six months of life, your baby may start to show signs of stranger anxiety. She may suddenly become uncomfortable around unfamiliar faces. She may no longer want Grandma to hold her or may be unhappy being passed around from person to person at the next neighborhood gathering. She may cry and cling to you. In some cases, she may only want to be held by mom.

While it is annoying, stranger anxiety is completely normal, and it usually passes in a few months. We suggest that you follow your baby's lead on who she wants to be with. Don't try to force her into Grandpa's arms just to make him feel better—it'll just make your baby feel more anxious and cling more tightly to you.

> ### Jamie's Solution
> Jamie's daughter cried in his arms whenever his wife went out for a few hours. Jamie's solution was to give her to someone else for a few minutes, whereupon his daughter's crying escalated to full-blown wailing! When she came back to Jamie she merely whimpered. Jamie wasn't mom, but he was at least better than anyone else!

Remind Grandpa that it's not personal; it's just a phase that she'll outgrow. She will be running to give him hugs and kisses soon enough.

Despite the onset of stranger anxiety, the six-month well-child visit is when Jamie routinely gives parents his famous Date Night prescription. It is a prescription given to the parents from the baby and signed by Jamie, reminding them to go out on a date at least once a month. After six months of continuous child care—a relationship that is constantly focused on the baby—it is time to start rekindling the relationship between the parents. Babies are wonderful, but the family unit is important, too. As parents, you have to remember that life does not always revolve around the baby, and that she can occasionally survive without you.

Vaccines at Six Months

This visit will provide boosters for the eight recommended vaccines given at the two-and four-month well visits. Once again, those vaccines are:

- Haemophilus influenza type B (HIB)
- Pneumococcal vaccine
- Diphtheria, tetanus, and acellular pertussis (DTaP)
- Hepatitis B
- Inactivated polio (IPV) and
- Rotavirus

Rotavirus is an oral vaccine and hepatitis B, DTaP, and IPV can be combined into one needle, which means your baby only needs three injections and one vaccine by mouth.

Depending on the actual brand of vaccines used, there may be some variation in the above recommendations. Certain brands of HIB vaccine do not require a six-month booster. In addition, both hepatitis B and inactivated polio can be given at any time between six and eighteen months. Thus, if you are immunizing under an alternative schedule, you can reasonably delay these booster vaccines. However, as they are both part of a combination vaccine that includes DTaP, and the third booster of DTaP is recommended at this visit, it is common to receive them now.

In addition to the above vaccines, if your baby's six-month well visit falls during flu season (October through March), the CDC recommends getting an influenza vaccine at this time with a booster dose one month later. There are two types of flu vaccine for children ages six to thirty-five months: with preservative (thimerosal) and without. The CDC feels that the amount of thimerosal (a mercury derivative) in the vaccine with preservative is insignificant and recommends either one. However, if you have concerns about thimerosal in your baby's flu vaccine, you can ask for preservative-free flu vaccine. It is more expensive, so fewer doctors stock it, but it is available. Ask your doctor if he knows who is offering the preservative-free vaccine (if he doesn't have any) or you may need to call around to find it. Full details on these and all vaccines given in the first year of life, plus information on the issues surrounding thimerosal, can be found in Chapter 13.

If you had any concerns regarding your baby's reaction to the vaccines given at the last check-up, please bring them up with your physician at the beginning of this visit. He might remind you that the reaction falls within the normal spectrum or review with you how to use medications to alleviate pain or fevers. Alternatively, he might suggest changing the pattern of vaccinations to help him determine which vaccine is associated with which reaction.

Remember that you do not have to follow the recommended schedule. You can request that the vaccines be given using an alternative schedule. Many parents are hesitant to have multiple vaccines given to their child all at once and are more accepting of the process if the vaccines are spread out, with maybe one or two vaccines given at one visit and the rest one or two weeks later. Also, whether to vaccinate your child is your choice. Discuss your concerns and options with your physician.

9

Your Baby at Nine Months

The nine-month milestone is a joy for parents. At this point your baby is coming into his own as a person. He consistently sits up by himself, which automatically creates a different sort of interaction with others. Instead of needing to be held, he can support himself and interact with you across the table, just like everyone else in the world. As his verbal skills start taking off, he'll begin holding babble "conversations" with you. And as he learns to crawl and pull himself up to stand, he is becoming mobile. The last three months of baby's first year feel like a fast toboggan ride down a snowy slope—both fun and a little scary!

Major Topic at Nine Months

The major topic at nine months is gross motor skills. This is usually the area where your child is making the most progress. Remember that there is a wide range of skills in children at this age. Some children have already started walking by this time, while others are still crawling or scooting along, yet both can be on normal developmental trajectories. However, most children at this point have some basic skills.

Rolling Over and Sitting

Most babies can roll over two and three times in a row and will use this as a way to get to objects they can't reach. In addition, most children are able to sit up unsupported, holding themselves upright for minutes at a time. Your baby may fall when he tips too far (watch his head on those backward falls), but he has learned to catch himself with his arms. He might have even learned how to get from a lying position into a sitting position without assistance.

If your baby is unable to sit up unsupported and roll over by nine months of age, you should request a developmental evaluation from your doctor.

Crawling

The next major skill is crawling. Your baby needs to be comfortable on his stomach (so give him lots of tummy time!), and then he will learn to get up on his hands and knees. It is interesting to watch him figure out what to do next. He has to learn how to balance on three limbs while moving the fourth. This usually requires rocking first, to shift his weight, and then moving one arm to a new position. Soon he will be alternating arms and legs like a champion and moving around the house *very* quickly. You'll be amazed at how fast babies can crawl!

An interesting note on crawling: Ever since physicians have been recommending that babies sleep only on their backs, more children skip the crawling stage entirely. While it is still a very small minority of children (under 5 percent), it is more than was seen fifteen years ago. Our theory is that with less tummy time exposure, some children never learn the precursor skills to crawling and find other means of mobility such as scooting on their bottoms.

Climbing

After crawling comes climbing. Steps and stools that are about twelve inches high are the perfect height for him to explore. The top of the step or stool will be at eye level when he's sitting, and he can sit back and reach his hands out toward it. With time, he will learn to rock forward and pull himself up so that he is standing next to the step. Finally, he will learn to lift a leg up and climb up onto the new surface.

Be very careful here. He won't understand the concept of an edge right away, which makes it very easy for him to fall down. This is a great time to teach him how to come down off a ledge safely. Once he masters how to reverse the steps of climbing and back off a height (tummy down, legs going down first), he will be able to transfer that skill and go down stairs safely. It is incredibly scary to see a child going down a flight of stairs face first, worrying that he will fall forward before you can catch him.

Standing
Your baby's next major motor skill is pulling himself up to a standing position. He will transfer the concept of pulling himself up a short height like a step, to a larger height like a couch or a chair. This skill is often developed first in the crib. The vertical railings are extremely easy to hang onto, and the top horizontal railing is often at the ideal height for baby to hold onto to fully stand up. (If your baby sleeps in a crib and is pulling himself up to stand, it's time to move the mattress to the lowest setting so that he can't climb over the top rail.)

Cruising to Walking
After standing will come cruising, which is simply supported walking by holding onto objects. Again cribs, as well as couches and coffee tables, are at a perfect height to practice this skill. And finally your baby will be truly walking, first using fingers or push toys for balance, and then going solo. This probably won't happen until around his first birthday, but it is a major milestone and a point of pride—for you and for him.

Common Questions at Nine Months

Is my baby gaining enough weight?

Parents often wonder why their baby isn't gaining weight as fast as he did in the past. This is totally normal. If you look at the growth curves, you'll notice that they start to flatten out after six months of age. This means that even though a baby may gain a pound in one or two weeks in the first month of life, it might take four to six weeks to gain a pound at nine months of age (and eight to ten weeks after their third birthday!)

If you are exclusively breastfeeding, remember that your baby might look underweight if your doctor is using the CDC growth curves from the year 2000. Those curves were made from data that included both breastfed and formula-fed babies. When evaluated according to those charts, babies who are exclusively breastfed appear overweight in their first six months and underweight in the next six months. This is true even for exclusively breastfed babies who start supplementary food after six months of age.

How many teeth should my baby have now?

This varies by child. Some babies have six or eight teeth by this point while other perfectly healthy children don't get any teeth until after their first birthday. In general, the central four incisors arrive first, at around six to nine months, and the lateral four incisors usually arrive a month or two later. Next come the first molars between twelve and eighteen months, and then the canine teeth between the molars and the incisors at sixteen to twenty-four months. Finally, the second molars arrive around the second birthday, completing the set of twenty baby teeth. Delayed arrival of teeth usually runs in families and only rarely suggests a medical problem.

When is my baby's soft spot going to go away?

The soft spot, also known as the anterior fontanel, is an opening between bones of the skull. These bones have interlocking sutures that mesh together, like the teeth of a zipper. However, when several of the skull bones come together at one point, they leave a wider opening. The smaller opening is at the junction of three bones at the back of the head and disappears before six months. The anterior fontanel is the larger opening at the junction of four bones at the top of the head and disappears more slowly. For most children this soft spot disappears somewhere between twelve and eighteen months, but in rare cases, it might persist longer. Your doctor will be monitoring your baby's fontanel, head circumference, weight, and height at every well visit and can let you know if there is a problem.

Growth and Development at Nine Months

Along with the gross motor development mentioned above, your baby should also be developing fine motor skills. The most obvious of these is the pincer grasp. He should have progressed from the palmar grasp at six months of age to a three-fingered pincer grasp (thumb, index, and middle fingers) at this age, and then to a two-fingered pincer grasp (thumb and index finger) before his first birthday. One way of encouraging this progression is to put small but safe foods on his highchair tray. A classic parental choice is unsweetened O-shaped cereals which are easy to clean up if spilled but not a choking hazard because they turn to mush quickly in the mouth.

As for language skills, your baby will continue to produce nonsense sounds like "ba ba ba." While a few rare children actually use a sound as a word, most have still not made the connection between certain sounds and meanings at that point. You can actively encourage this connection by repeating sounds back to him in an enthusiastic manner and pointing to the objects they represent. So, if you point at a bird and say "buh, buh, bird," he will eventually realize that the sound is linked to the object and will try to make it himself.

One way to combine the fine motor skills with language is to teach your baby some simple sign language. Did you know that your baby's language comprehension far exceeds his speaking ability? In addition, his ability to manipulate his hands exceeds his ability to use his vocal cords to make words. Because of this, some parents teach their babies sign language, giving them an early way to communicate. There are books and websites available to teach you how to do it, if you are interested. Do an online search with the words *baby sign language* or ask your local librarian for suggestions. While most parents only teach their babies to sign a few words, dedicated parents have sometimes found that their baby can develop a vocabulary of twenty to fifty signed words before they can say ten words.

Some babies are especially slow to develop speech. There are many reasons a child may have delayed speech—some serious, others unknown and benign. One of the huge benefits of teaching your baby sign language is that it lowers his frustration at not being able to tell you what he wants and not being able to communicate as well as he wishes. If your child happens to have delayed speech, imagine how much less frustrated he will be if he is able to communicate with you clearly through sign language.

Jen knows a little boy who was not speaking at three years of age, whose parents taught him hundreds of signs. He's receiving speech therapy now for his delayed speech problem, but he's a lucky little boy that his parents taught him so many signs. He would have been incredibly frustrated to go so long without being able to tell his parents all that he had to say.

Safety Concerns at Nine Months

Once again, you need to look at your house from a baby's perspective in order to update your childproofing. This time, try moving around with your head at different levels to see what he sees. The crawling baby will see objects at about 12 inches off the ground but a child who can pull up to standing might be able to reach over his head to three feet. At nine months, objects on coffee tables and low shelves become more interesting, and bottom drawers in the kitchen are fair game. We suggest having as few areas as possible remain off-limits, so you don't have to say "no!" all day long. It is okay to put baby latches on a few drawers and cabinets to keep things safe, but if everything is locked up, he will get frustrated as his natural sense of curiosity and his desire to explore are thwarted.

If your baby is able to cruise around furniture or walk with a rolling toy, be prepared for him to fall. All babies fall. It is a normal part of learning to walk. They usually fall backward onto their bottoms, as they quickly learn that it is the safest way to get down. Occasionally, however, they will fall forward. This is especially scary on stairs, which is why it is good to teach them to go backward down stairs and off chairs and beds. It is also scary if they hit their heads on something. The corners of hearths around fireplaces or the edges of furniture can easily cause cuts that require sutures. Many parents choose to temporarily cover sharp or hard corners with foam until their baby is walking more steadily.

Some children weigh more than twenty pounds by this

If you have a fireplace or a wood-burning stove, put a gate or fence around it to protect baby from getting burned. You should also buy a carbon monoxide detector in case the outflow vent becomes obstructed.

age, and parents wonder if it is now safe to allow the car seat to face forward. The answer is *no*. Car seats should remain rear-facing until the child weighs more than twenty pounds *and* is past his first birthday. However, most infant carrier car seats are only rated up to twenty-two pounds, so if your baby weighs more than the recommended weight for your infant car seat, you'll need to upgrade to an upright, rear-facing car seat at this point (usually called a "convertible car seat"). After his first birthday, this upright car seat can be turned to face forward.

A new safety concern at this age is lead exposure. There are national recommendations for screening all children at ages one and two to determine the level of lead in their blood, but your physician might recommend screening your baby earlier if he falls into a high-risk category. Some activities that increase your baby's risk for elevated lead include:

- Living in or frequently visiting a house built before 1950
- Living in or frequently visiting a house built before 1978 that is being remodeled
- Living in a house with lead plumbing
- Living in a high-risk neighborhood (more than 27 percent of the houses were built before 1950)
- Having siblings, friends, or playmates with high lead levels
- Frequently putting foreign objects such paint chips in his mouth
- Having family members whose work or hobbies regularly expose them to materials containing lead, such as welding, automotive repair, batteries, construction sites and more

The actual lead screening test will involve a finger prick to draw a few drops of blood to send to the lab. This is usually very well tolerated by the baby. Remember to wash your baby's hand before the poke. If his hand has dust or dirt on it that is contaminated with lead, this might give a falsely elevated reading. If the first reading is high, it is usually followed up with a second test, with blood drawn from a vein in the arm. If that sample is still elevated, your physician will discuss your options with you, both for treatment, which is rarely needed these days, and for prevention.

As always, stop smoking if you are currently smoking, make sure the smoke detectors, carbon monoxide detectors, and fire extinguishers work, and check the hot water temperature again to make sure that it is around 120 degrees Fahrenheit. Also, make sure you have the poison control stickers prominently posted in your house and carry some with you just in case you need the number while away from home.

Recurring Issues at Nine Months

Your baby should have a wide and varied diet by this age as you actively expose him to more and more new foods and spices. Remember to avoid honey and cow's milk until after his first birthday. Many parents also avoid potentially allergenic foods, such as nuts, until then as well. Please continue to read to your baby daily, continue to supplement with vitamin D if he is taking less than sixteen ounces of formula a day, and supplement with fluoride if your water supply is not fluoridated. Finally, recall that the American Academy of Pediatrics (AAP) recommends that mothers continue to breastfeed their babies

> There is no medical concern that arises with the baby waking up to eat three or four times at night. This is actually a common pattern in cultures around the world; however, because we live in a busy, fast-paced society that prizes independence, this pattern is usually seen as abnormal. If you are comfortable with your sleeping situation, there is no need to change it.

until they are at least a year old (and longer if mutually agreeable to mom and baby).

Sleep is still a contentious topic at this age. Some children sleep nine or ten hours in a row at this age, while others still wake three or more times during the night. Needless to say, this can be very hard on the parents and lead to frustration about the best way to improve their child's sleep habits.

One rule to remember about sleep issues is this: Never make a hasty decision or try to "discuss" the issue in the middle of the night. We are never at our best, let alone our most rational, when pulled out of bed for the fourth time in one night by a crying baby. Find a quiet time during the day to consider your options together and come up with a plan as to how you want to proceed.

Vaccines at Nine Months

There are no scheduled vaccines at this visit. If you have previously chosen an alternative schedule and delayed some of the two-, four-, or six-month vaccines, your baby may have some catch-up vaccines to receive at this time. In addition, if this well visit is scheduled between the months of October and March and you did not get the flu vaccine at an earlier visit, the CDC recommends getting an influenza vaccine at this time with a booster dose one month later. Remember that if you have concerns about the preservative thimerosal in your baby's flu vaccine, you can ask for preservative-free flu vaccine. Full details on this and all vaccines given in the first year of life, plus information on the issues surrounding thimerosal, can be found in Chapter Thirteen.

Your Baby at Twelve Months

10

Congratulations! You have survived your baby's first year. Her birthday party is more a celebration for you than for her. While she has grown from a helpless newborn into a walking, talking "big girl," you have matured from a novice into an experienced and seasoned parent. It has been a tremendous year of growth and development, for her and for you, and you both have a lot to be proud of. Pat yourself on the back and get ready for the next steps of the journey.

Major Topic at Twelve Months

The major topic at twelve months is language development. By this time, your baby's nonsense sounds like "ma ma ma" or "ba ba ba" will likely have developed into a few words. "Word" is loosely defined at this stage of life. If she uses the same sound again and again for a particular object or verb, that's a word. So if she says "uh" for *up* or "ba" for *ball* or *box* or *banana* and says it consistently, that counts as a word. On average, she will have one or two words by twelve months of age, usually *mama* or *dada* and one other word.

In contrast to her spoken language, her language *comprehension* consists of dozens of words and phrases. She understands far more than she can say. She knows the names of mom and dad and other important caretakers. She can understand the concept of someone coming home from work and will look at the front door anticipating their arrival. She can follow simple commands and will (usually) respond when you call to her. She is very aware of language.

This disparity between comprehension and expression—between words understood and words she can say—can be a source of frustration for your baby. As mentioned earlier, many parents find that teaching their baby sign language at this stage is helpful in bridging that gap and lessening their baby's frustration. When a baby can express her needs via signs instead of grunts, she feels (and is) better understood and is better able to control her environment.

Babies are amazing in so many ways, one of which is that they are programmed to learn languages and will learn whatever they hear. She can also learn multiple languages simultaneously. Jamie knows of a family where the father only spoke Swedish to the children while the mother spoke only Serbian to them, and the parents then spoke to each other in English. The children grew up fluent in English (because they grew up in upstate New York) and are conversational in the other two languages.

If you want to give your baby the gift of multiple languages, you have to truly expose her to the languages on a regular and consistent basis. She can't just hear the words now and then when you remember to speak Spanish or French or any other language to them. You have to consistently talk and read to her every day, ask her what she wants for breakfast, and remind her to put on her coat in the second language. And you have to be patient. In general, children with multiple languages are delayed on language skills at twelve to eighteen months but are fully caught up in both languages by two or two and a half years.

Common Questions at the Twelve-Month Visit

Should I brush my baby's teeth yet?

At this point in time, the goal with teeth brushing is to create a habit and routine with your baby's teeth, not to do a perfect job with dental care. So we suggest that you introduce a toothbrush at this age and let your baby chew on it. We don't recommend adding toothpaste right away (unless she insists) because some children hate the taste of toothpaste and then refuse the toothbrush because it is associated with the unpleasant taste.

A few weeks or more after you've introduced the toothbrush, you can add toothpaste to the brush. She will likely swallow it, but that is not a big concern now. In a few more months you can let her brush, but also insist on letting an adult brush for her as well. And finally, you can introduce floss between eighteen and twenty-four months, either as a string or in a flossing pick. Again, the floss is there to create a habit, not because it is needed for her teeth yet; most children will have large spaces between their teeth until they're much older.

If you can manage this routine twice a day, or even better, after every meal, you are way ahead of the game. Most parents are happy to get their baby's teeth brushed once a day as part of the nighttime ritual. There is no easy answer as to when you should have your baby's teeth examined by a dentist. While some dentists are willing to see children as young as one or two years old, most ask parents to wait until after the child's third birthday, and some don't want to see your child until age four or five.

The major goal of dental care at this age is making sure that no food or sugary liquid sits next to the teeth all night long. For that purpose you can simply wipe her teeth with a cloth. You should also be aware of *early childhood caries* (ECC), also known as baby cavities. The most important way to prevent your baby from getting cavities is to make sure that she does not fall asleep with a bottle of formula in her mouth. Breastfeeding babies can also have problems if they nurse to sleep, so we recommend that you unlatch the baby while he is drowsy but before he actually falls asleep.

As with so many other things, Mom's health affects baby's health in this area, so some babies are at a higher risk for ECC if mom has had lots of cavities in the past, and especially if she currently has any decay. To help protect your baby from a similar fate, take good care of your teeth. The AAP makes these recommendations for mom to prevent ECC in her children:

- Brush thoroughly twice a day with a fluoride toothpaste.
- Floss and use a fluoride rinse once daily.
- Avoid sugary drinks during the first thirty months of your baby's life.
- Have your teeth cleaned every six months and any cavity filled.
- Do not share spoons with your baby or clean a pacifier with your mouth—that is how the bacteria that cause decay are transferred to baby.
- Chew gum sweetened with xylitol—four pieces a day. (In studies xylitol has been shown to decrease the rate of ECC).

The AAP also recommends that children who are at higher risk see a dentist six months after their first tooth erupts or at twelve months of age, whichever comes first. There are early signs of ECC that your dentist can look for, and he can instruct you on ways to prevent your child from getting cavities. ECC is more prevalent than asthma, but it is very preventable with good oral hygiene habits. This is a really great subject to discuss with your dentist when you are in for your regular cleanings.

Growth and Development at Twelve Months

By twelve months of age, your baby should be sitting and crawling well, and will probably be pulling herself up to a standing position. She should have a good pincer grasp and be able to feed herself with her fingers. She might be able to feed herself with a spoon or fork, but that varies by child. She might be walking by this point, taking a few steps by herself, but many babies don't walk until after their first birthday. If your child is not sitting well or lacks mobility (meaning she is unable to do at least one of the following: walk, crawl, or scooch around on her bottom), then she needs to be evaluated for a motor delay.

Over the next several months, your baby will pick up many new skills. She will begin walking well and will be able to navigate around the house. She will probably start climbing onto stairs and furniture, and, if inclined, might use a chair to climb onto the kitchen table. Although this may give you a heart attack, she will be very proud of herself. She will develop better fine motor control of her hands and may start scribbling with a crayon. And as discussed above, she will become more verbal and expressive in her wants and needs. Although temper tantrums are still a ways off, the word "no" will soon appear as part of her vocabulary.

Safety Concerns at Twelve Months

With your baby's improved mobility, you'll need to protect her from even more hazards in the house. The big areas of concern are climbing and running. If your baby is adventurous, she may want to explore heights. Some children figure out that if they push chairs over to tables or counters they can climb up onto them. So, whereas in the past you might have been able to cut an apple and leave the knife on the counter, now your baby might be able to grab the knife with relatively little trouble. Agile children can learn to climb onto the counters and open up the high cupboards, so you'll need to move dangerous objects even higher.

As for other risks, many of your particular concerns will be determined by your baby's personality and abilities, both in and out of the house. Be careful if your baby is both curious *and* fast. She may learn to open doors on her own, so she could be able leave the house to explore outdoors without your knowledge. In this case, you will need some sort of latch or chain high on the door to prevent her from going outside unsupervised. If she learns how to manipulate locks, she may lock herself in a bedroom or bathroom, so make sure you have the proper tools to open household doors from the outside. And don't rely on screens in windows to prevent your child from falling, because they are not sufficient to bear the weight of a heavy child who leans against them.

Now that your baby is a year old, you might be able to turn her car seat around so it is forward facing, but only *if* she weighs more than twenty pounds. Turning it around is not required, however. Many upright car seats are allowed to be used as rear-facing seats until the child is weighs more than thirty pounds, and many experts feel that rear-facing car seats are generally safer than forward-facing ones. So our recommendation is to keep your baby rear-facing as long as both you and she can tolerate it.

As always, stop smoking if you are currently smoking; make sure the smoke detectors, fire extinguishers, and carbon monoxide detectors work; and check the hot water temperature to make sure that it is no hotter than about 120 degrees Fahrenheit. Make sure you have the poison control stickers prominently posted in your house and carry some with you just in case you need the number while away from home.

Finally, your physician will recommend screening your child for lead exposure at this time. This will involve a finger poke to draw a few drops of blood to send to the lab. Remember to wash your baby's hand before the poke. If her hand has dust or dirt on it that is contaminated with lead, the dirt might give a falsely elevated reading. If the first reading is high, it is usually followed up with a second test, with blood drawn from a vein in the arm. If that sample is still elevated, your physician will discuss your options with you, both for treatment, which is rarely needed these days, and for prevention.

Recurring Issues at Twelve Months
- -

Now that your baby has reached her first birthday, you can start experimenting with some of the "forbidden" foods. Honey can now be safely added to her diet, as can cow's milk. It is appropriate to try other foods on the potential allergy list, such as peanut butter, egg whites, or fish. Remember to try just one new food a day. In the unlikely case that there is a severe reaction, such as breathing problems or a whole-body rash, consult your physician. Don't be too quick to blame the new food if a mild reaction, such as stomach upset or a diaper rash, occurs at the same time a food is introduced. It is best to wait until a reaction happens twice before declaring your baby intolerant of a certain food. And remember, a childhood reaction need not be a ban for life on that particular food. Many children are able to handle previously intolerable foods when they are older. (See Chapter Fifteen for more information on feeding your baby.)

Recall that the American Academy of Pediatrics (AAP) recommends that mothers continue to breastfeed their babies until they are at least a year old (and longer if mutually agreeable to mom and baby). This means that you do not *need* to wean your baby now. Worldwide, the average length of breastfeeding is over four years, and many mothers in the United States continue to nurse their babies until they are two or three years old. You will continue to give her comfort, nutrition, and protection from infections for as long as you are nursing. We recommend continuing to breastfeed your baby for as long as both you and she are comfortable with the process.

Please continue reading to your baby daily, and continue to supplement with fluoride for tooth protection if your water supply is not fluoridated. The recommendation for vitamin D is only for the first year of life so you can stop giving that supplement now if you wish. If you are still having issues with your baby waking up more than once a night, please review Chapter Fourteen for suggestions.

Vaccines at Twelve Months

The next several well-child visits come with several booster vaccines, repetitions of those that were scheduled at two, four, and six months of age, plus several new vaccines.

Twelve- to Eighteen- Month Vaccines are:

- HIB
- Pneumococcal
- DTaP
- MMR
- Varicella
- Hepatitis A

The booster vaccines are the HIB and pneumococcal vaccines, recommended at twelve to fifteen months, and the DTaP vaccine, recommended at fifteen to eighteen months, though DTaP can be given at twelve months of age under certain circumstances. There is a combination HIB/DTaP vaccine available that saves one needle for your child, but, as of this writing, it contains a trace amount of thimerosal introduced during the manufacturing process. While the CDC considers the trace of mercury contained in the vaccine insignificant, it is up to you to decide if you would rather have an extra needle or the trace of the thimerosal preservative.

The new vaccines are the measles, mumps, and rubella (MMR) vaccine; the varicella or chickenpox vaccine; and the hepatitis A vaccine. Both the MMR and varicella vaccines are recommended at twelve to fifteen months and can be combined into one shot. Unfortunately, the combined vaccine, which comes under trade name Proquad, is reported to cause an increased risk of fever—specifically, one in five people who receive the combined vaccine will get a mild fever, as opposed one in ten among those who do not. Again, the decision is yours as to whether you would prefer the slightly higher risk of fever or an extra needle.

The hepatitis A vaccine is given in a series of two injections scheduled at least six months apart. The easiest way to arrange that timing is to give the first hepatitis A vaccine at the twelve-month well-child visit and the second at the eighteen-month well-child visit.

In addition, if this well visit is scheduled sometime between October and March, and you did not get the flu vaccine at an earlier visit, the CDC recommends getting an influenza vaccine at this time, with a booster dose one month later. If you have concerns about the preservative thimerosal in your baby's flu vaccine, you can ask for preservative-free flu vaccine.

Remember that you have the option of choosing an alternative schedule for the vaccines. In one scenario, your baby could receive five needles at the twelve-month visit (HIB, pneumococcal, MMR/varicella, hepatitis A, and influenza) and then the influenza booster a month later. One reasonable alternative would be to spread the schedule out slightly by giving three vaccines at each visit. For example, you could give the first influenza, hepatitis A, and HIB vaccines at the twelve-month well visit and then the second influenza, pneumococcal, and MMR/Varicella combined vaccine one month later. You have to return for the second influenza vaccination anyway, and the recommended schedule ranges from twelve to fifteen months for all the vaccines mentioned.

Full details on these and all other vaccines given in the first year of life, plus information on the issues surrounding thimerosal, can be found in Chapter Thirteen.

Part Three

Hot Topics

What are the benefits of breastfeeding? What are the risks and benefits of various vaccines? Will my baby ever sleep through the night? What do I do if my baby has a fever? You'll find answers to these questions and more in Chapters Eleven through Seventeen. They cover a variety of important issues—some controversial—that may be mentioned earlier in the book, but that warrant more in-depth discussion. Feel free to read these chapters separately at any time during your baby's first year because they cover longer term issues. In addition, these chapters can be revisited as your baby grows to give you more ideas for how to handle the matters in question.

Breastfeeding

Breastfeeding can be an empowering experience for a mom. It's incredible to have your body create everything your baby needs to grow and thrive during his first six to twelve months of life. You may feel like you have a new superpower! And yet, in actuality, breastfeeding is really just a normal process.

Normal it may be, but there is something sincerely magical about watching your baby nurse or smile up at you from your breast. By breastfeeding you are giving your baby the best possible start in life. Not only are you giving him the perfect food that benefits him nutritionally as well as improves his immune system, you are also forming a strong bond with him. The more we research it, the more we learn that breast milk is an incredible substance that no one can come close to replicating.

For some women, breastfeeding is an absolute breeze, coming very naturally with little to no problems at all. For others there will be a learning curve. We'll talk about some possible bumps in the breastfeeding road in this chapter, as well as what to do if or when they occur. We'll also offer suggestions on how to make breastfeeding a success. You do so many things while pregnant to ensure that your baby will grow to be as healthy as possible;

the best way to continue to do that after baby is born is to breastfeed.

Breast Really *Is* Best

Breast milk is truly nature's perfect food. Your body makes it uniquely for *your* baby. It is full of your immunities and antibodies to help protect your baby from illness and disease. It is the perfect balance of fat, carbohydrates, and protein, and it alters as your baby grows to meet his changing nutritional needs. It is easily digested by your baby and is excreted as non-smelly poop (which is a blessing you only really realize after baby has started solids and things get stinky!). No one can manufacture its equal.

Almost all women can breastfeed. A small percentage of women do not produce enough milk to exclusively breastfeed their babies, but they can continue to nurse while supplementing with donor breast milk (from another mom) or formula to make up the difference. Some women cannot breastfeed because a required medication or an infection passes into their milk and would be harmful for their babies. But overall, most women can breastfeed.

> ### In Case You Were Wondering . . .
> Breast size has nothing to do with how much milk a woman can produce. Small-breasted or large-breasted, most women can make plenty of milk to support their growing babies. Size does affect how much milk is stored and waiting for your baby. So a smaller-breasted woman may need to nurse more often to keep her supply up.

Breastfeeding benefits your baby in a multitude of ways. Breastfed babies get sick less often because breast milk contains living immune cells that help protect your baby. Research shows that for every ten babies who are exclusively breastfed for at least three months, their families will have twenty fewer doctor's visits, six fewer prescriptions, and two fewer days in the hospital in the first year of life. And that is just for three illnesses—vomiting and diarrhea, ear infections, and lower respiratory infections. If you extend the research to other medical illnesses, the benefits are even greater. (One study found that during a six month period a group of formula-fed infants incurred $68,000 in medical expenses, while an equal number of their breastfeeding counterparts had only $4,000.) If you have a family history of allergies, breast milk will decrease your baby's risk of developing food allergies, asthma, or eczema by 30 percent.

Breastfeeding also benefits mothers. Not only is it a warm, loving experience that requires mom to relax and have quiet time several times a day, it also has impressive health benefits for her. Breastfeeding moms lose pregnancy weight more easily due to the extra calories they burn each day as their bodies make milk. This might mean as much as a six-pound difference at six months. Those who had gestational diabetes are also less likely to develop type 2 diabetes later on if they breastfeed their babies. Breastfeeding stimulates the uterus to contract and return to its normal size, lessening postpartum bleeding. Exclusive breastfeeding delays the return of ovulation and menstruation. And just the knowledge that she is

> *Exclusive breastfeeding* means baby only receives breast milk, whether directly from the breast or in a bottle for the first six months of life, and then only breast milk and solids after that. There is no supplementation with artificial milks when a baby is exclusively breastfed.

doing the most she can to ensure a healthy baby is a benefit to mom because she will face less stress and have lower medical costs, too.

Mothers who breastfeed also enjoy a decreased risk of ovarian, uterine, and breast cancers, as well as a decreased risk of osteoporosis. The research on breast cancer is particularly impressive. The actual risk decreases in relation to how long a mom nurses her baby, going from a few percent decrease for nursing just a few months to a full 50 percent decrease for nursing more than two and a half years! Just so you know, the benefit is cumulative, and is even greater if you breastfeed subsequent children.

Nursing your baby is an empowering experience for parents. Realizing the wonder of your body creating a food that can solely support your baby's health and development for the first six to twelve months of his life can help a woman feel more confident in herself as a mother. Fathers can also feel more confident as they support moms in breastfeeding their children, knowing that their babies are getting the very best and marveling at mom's newfound superpower to feed and comfort.

A Place for Partners

How can dads or partners be involved? Here's a list of things you can do to support mom and bond with your baby.

- Help mom stay hydrated. When she sits down to nurse, bring her a glass of water.
- Encourage mom to get help from a lactation expert if she's having problems.
- Stay nearby. While baby is nursing, talk to him, smile at him. Be a part of the nursing session when you can.
- Burp your baby when he's done nursing.
- Do a fair share of baby's other caretaking. Change diapers, give baby a bath, feed him once he starts eating solid food, rock him to sleep, take him for walks in a carrier, and hold him. These are all wonderful ways to create a strong bond with your baby.

Above all, be supportive. While breastfeeding is natural and instinctive, it is also a learned skill. It can take a while for both mom and baby to figure out how to nurse smoothly and painlessly. There may be tears and doubts in the first few days and some mothers panic when their baby loses weight, even when they are reassured that it is completely normal. Breastfeeding succeeds in an encouraging environment. Your love and support are vital to ensure that success. Give mom the confidence she needs to continue, even if the going is rough, by having faith that she can do it and reminding her that it will get easier.

Getting Started

Babies come wired to breastfeed; studies have shown that babies will instinctually make their way to mom's breast from her tummy and latch on to start nursing in the first hours after birth. The best way to begin your breastfeeding relationship with your baby is during the first hour of his life. Immediately following his birth, hold your baby skin-to-skin on your abdomen or chest. (Both mom and dad should hold him skin-to-skin as often as possible afterwards as well.) After you've spent time gazing in awe, bring him to your breast to nurse. Not only is that what he needs, it is also what you need to stimulate your body to start making milk.

> **The AAP recommends that babies be exclusively breastfed for the first six months of life, and that nursing continue for at least the first full year and for as long past a year as desired by mother and child.**

It will take a few days for your milk to come in, but in the meantime your baby will be getting colostrum. Colostrum is liquid gold, as it is a golden-colored fluid rich in antibodies. This incredible stuff (which cannot be manufactured) passes on all of your immunities to your baby. It also has a laxative effect that helps baby get the meconium, that sticky newborn poop, out of his system. Getting those bowels moving also helps reduce the chances that your baby will be jaundiced.

Nursing your baby as often as possible—every two to three hours at first—means he will get plenty of colostrum and your breasts will get the signal to start making milk. You may need to encourage your sleepy baby to nurse early on. Rub his back or feet to keep him awake while nursing. When your milk comes in, continuing to nurse frequently helps prevent engorged breasts. If you do experience engorgement (breasts being uncomfortably full) and baby is asleep, you might want to hand express or pump to ease the discomfort.

How Often Should Baby Nurse?

As often as he wants. Usually you'll end up nursing between eight and twelve times within a twenty-four hour period. For some babies it'll be less, for some it'll be more. Once solid food is a consistent part of his diet, you may find that baby will nurse slightly less. But breast milk will continue to be the mainstay of baby's diet for most of the first year of his life.

You may also find that your breasts will leak early on. To stop the leaking, simply apply pressure to your nipple(s). You may leak out of one side while nursing your baby on the other side, or you may leak out of both breasts from time to time when you're not nursing. Wearing breast pads in your bra (cloth or disposable) helps to soak up the extra breast milk so you're less likely to have wet marks on your shirt.

There are things you can do ahead of time to prepare your nipples for nursing. Spreading purified lanolin on your nipples is a great way to get them "conditioned" for the work ahead. It's also a good way to soothe sore nipples once you've started nursing. Your hospital may have samples that you can use, and you can buy it at many stores in the baby product section. Don't worry if your baby gets some in his mouth while nursing, it won't hurt him.

Latching On

Getting a good latch, or attachment, between the baby's mouth and the mom's breast is imperative and the only way to avoid sore nipples. How do you know you're getting a good latch? It doesn't hurt. How do you know you're not getting a good latch? It hurts.

Okay, that's really simplified, but true for the most part. Of course, you may have some tenderness when beginning to breast-feed as your nipples adjust (especially if you have sensitive skin), so it is possible that you'll be getting a good latch and still have some discomfort when you first start nursing. But after a few days, if the latch is good, then you should no longer be in pain. If you are in pain then something is wrong, and you should seek help from a lactation expert.

To ensure a good latch, you must position your baby properly. You should be tummy to tummy with your baby, so he doesn't have to turn his head to get to your breast. His head, shoulders, and hips should form a straight line. His head should tip back slightly, with his chin coming toward your breast. (You do not want the chin tucked in toward the neck because it's awfully hard to swallow in that position—try it.) You want to get baby to open his mouth really wide. Pull him in quickly to the breast, getting as much areola (the dark skin around your nipple) in his mouth as possible. More of the areola below your nipple should be in his mouth than that above the nipple. (See diagram.)

Mother's view, left breast

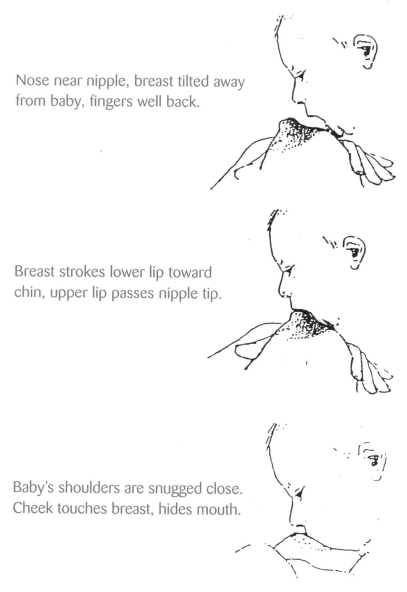

Nose near nipple, breast tilted away from baby, fingers well back.

Breast strokes lower lip toward chin, upper lip passes nipple tip.

Baby's shoulders are snugged close. Cheek touches breast, hides mouth.

Used with permission. Drawings © John Wiessinger; descriptive text © Diane Wiessinger

If your breasts are really full, your baby may have trouble latching on. Pump or hand express enough milk out to soften your breast so baby can more easily latch on. That will also prevent baby from being overwhelmed with too much milk when the letdown reflex occurs. The letdown reflex is also called the milk ejection reflex. When a baby starts nursing or when a mom hears a cue that the baby wants to nurse (and that can even be a different baby's crying), the body releases a surge of a hormone called oxytocin or pitocin (yes, the same hormone used to augment labor). This reflex causes the breast to squeeze the muscles around the milk glands and push the milk in the glands into the milk ducts. It leads to increased milk in the ducts and can sometimes overwhelm a nursing baby.

When you want to unlatch your baby, gently slide your finger into baby's mouth right alongside your nipple. Your finger will break the seal, helping to release your nipple. You may need to slide your finger in far enough to place it between baby's upper and lower gums so he will not clamp down on your nipple as you unlatch him.

Signs of a Bad Latch
- **pain while nursing**
- **blisters forming on end of nipples**
- **cracks on nipples and/or bleeding**

If any of these things happen, please ask for immediate assistance from a lactation consultant on staff at the hospital, through your doctor's office, or contact a La Leche League leader for help. Though painful, these problems are minor and fairly easy to overcome.

Nursing for Comfort

Babies have a natural need to suck beyond simply satisfying their hunger. As your breastfeeding relationship develops, you will notice times when baby is nursing for comfort rather than hunger. That's okay. It's wonderful in fact. Breastfeeding is a great way to comfort your sometimes-fussy baby. We do so many other things to comfort our babies—holding, kissing, rocking, walking, singing—that it's perfectly natural to add breastfeeding to our comforting bag of tricks.

Sometimes, however, mom needs a break, and it's okay to find another source of comfort for your baby. Dads can get very creative here. Jen's husband would comfort their babies with singing. Jamie would vacuum to comfort his first baby while his wife got some much-needed rest; the noise of the vacuum helped soothe their colicky son. (It's amazing the little tricks you'll discover on your parenting path!) See Chapter Fifteen for more ideas on ways to comfort your baby.

Nursing for your baby's comfort helps you have a happy baby. And as every parent knows, a happy baby means happy parents.

Still Eating (and Drinking) for Two

Now that you are postpartum, you may be very intent on getting back to your pre-pregnancy weight and size. Fortunately, breastfeeding burns calories and helps you lose weight! But you also need to know that this is not the time to go on a crash diet. If you do not eat enough, your body cannot make enough milk for your baby. Remember: Everything you eat and drink affects your milk, and your baby is taking in everything that you are eating and drinking. Try to consume a varied, healthy diet full of fresh foods. Drink lots of water. Just as when you were pregnant, it's best to avoid caffeine and sugar substitutes (saccharin, aspartame, etc.). One cup of coffee won't do any harm, but remember that your baby will be taking in the caffeine also, so try to limit your intake. The same goes for alcohol.

Some mothers wonder if what they eat might be upsetting their baby's system. While this can happen, it is actually uncommon. To find out whether this is happening to your baby, you'll have to do some detective work. First, document the pattern of bothersome symptoms for the baby, such as colic (the most common food concern) or excessive gas. Then you have to determine if a particular food makes the symptoms better or worse. The most common culprits are dairy foods (like milk, yogurt, and cheese) and gas-producing foods (like broccoli and cauliflower). While some moms notice a distinct link, most don't find a significant difference when they eliminate certain foods from their diets. Keep in mind that altering your diet won't have to last forever. You will be able to eat those foods again once you are no longer nursing.

Medications and Herbal Remedies

Always, always, always check with your doctor before taking any medication or herbal remedy—whether over-the-counter or prescription—when you are nursing. A few medications that are passed into breast milk can be harmful to your baby. Even if it's after-hours, call the doctor who's on call to find out if it's safe for you to take something. We cannot stress the importance of this enough. *Always* clear medicines and dietary supplements with your doctor before taking them. (See Appendix D at the end of this book for a list of common medications and information on whether they are safe to take while breastfeeding.)

Having said that, there are actually only a few medicines that require you to interrupt nursing, and most of those are obvious, such as chemotherapeutic agents for cancer. If your physician prescribes a medication that she says is incompatible with breastfeeding, ask if there are any other drugs you could take instead that are compatible. The fact is that almost every medicine passes into breast milk but usually in such small amounts that it is not significant for your baby. It is also true that most physicians are not trained in this area and are risk-averse. Rather than thoroughly investigate the medicine, they may simply advise that you temporarily not breastfeed. It's in your (and your baby's) best interest to seek out expert advice and even to get second and third opinions. See the Resources section for links to well-respected websites where you can research the risks of certain drugs in breast milk.

Tips to Help Make Breastfeeding a Success

1. Nurse within the first hour of life if you can. (You should be able to as long as baby has no immediate medical issues.)
2. Have skin-to-skin contact with your newborn. Place him on your bare chest in only a diaper and keep both of you warm with a blanket.
3. Give it time. Try it for a minimum of four weeks to insure enough time to learn and master this new skill; this should help you get through any problems and experience the painless ease and joy of nursing. It very likely will become the easiest thing you do!
4. Get help when you need it. Seek out the counsel of a lactation expert if you are having any problems at all. You can find them through your hospital, doctor's office, or the local chapter of La Leche League.
5. Surround yourself with supportive people. Get dad onboard, find a supportive physician, go to La Leche League meetings.
6. Nurse on demand whenever baby is hungry, not according to a feeding schedule. (That's a sure way to maintain a good milk supply, as well as a happier—a.k.a. not hungry—baby. And a happy baby means a happy mom.)

Myths About Breastfeeding

Many women are worried about certain issues when it comes to breastfeeding, and may make the decision to not breastfeed or to stop early based on false information. These are the most common reasons that we've heard.

I can't breastfeed because I'll be going back to work.

While many companies do not provide a supportive atmosphere for the nursing mother (not providing mom with time and a private place to pump or on-site day care so she can nurse her baby throughout the day), there are things you can do to keep your breastfeeding relationship going with your baby.

First of all, you could continue to nurse at nights and on weekends when you are home with your baby. (Your body will adjust to making enough milk and timing the milk to be ready before work, after work, and during the night.) Secondly, if you start pumping before you return to work, you will build up a supply of breast milk that you can store in the freezer for when you are away from your baby. Remember to introduce the bottle several weeks before your return to work. You can also talk to your boss to arrange a way that you can pump when you go back to work, for instance by getting access to an empty office at various points during the day. You might find it helpful to have a letter from your doctor saying that breast milk is medically necessary for your baby. If that doesn't work out, you might need to supplement with donor milk or formula when your baby is with his caregiver. Finally, if your job offers maternity leave, you could choose to nurse exclusively during that time; at the very least, that will give baby a great start of several weeks of breast milk.

Keep in mind that for a working mom, breastfeeding is an effective and wonderful way to reconnect with your baby when you've been away from each other all day. It's an immediate connection, physically and emotionally, that helps strengthen your bond even when you can't be together all day long.

I won't make enough milk because my breasts are too small.

Actually, breast size has nothing to do with how much milk you can produce. There is a very small chance that you might not produce enough milk, but the risk of that is the same for small- and large-breasted women.

It'll be so inconvenient. Formula will be much easier.

Though it can take some work at the very beginning to learn how to do something that you've never done before, once you have it mastered it's easy—perhaps the easiest thing you'll do as a mom. Bottle feeding, though perhaps easier to start, never gets any easier. Additionally, breast milk is always with you, always the right temperature, and always ready to serve. There is no need for the nursing mom to take anything along to feed her baby when out of the house. Formula feeding requires having clean bottles and nipples, measuring and mixing the formula and water, and getting the formula to the right temperature. And sometimes this must be done when you're stumbling around in the dark at 3 a.m. By the time you're done fixing the formula, you could have a *very* hungry and upset baby on your hands. With nursing you can feed your baby immediately, anywhere, anytime.

It's embarrassing to nurse. I don't want to do that in public.

It's certainly legitimate to feel that way, and nursing in public does take some practice, both in terms of doing it discreetly, as well as getting used to it emotionally and psychologically. You have a great option, though. If you are worried about nursing in public or if it makes you uncomfortable, then don't do it. You can always nurse your baby in private in your car or bring a bottle of pumped breast milk for him to drink while you are out. Fortunately, most moms find they have no problems nursing away from home.

Nursing in Public

Here are some suggestions for nursing in public.

- Drape a shawl or light blanket over your shoulder and baby for the most privacy.
- Use specially designed nursing tops that allow you to only uncover the bare minimum.

- If you do not have nursing tops, wear a T-shirt with a big button-up shirt layered over it like a jacket. You can discreetly lift your shirt to nurse, while keeping yourself covered with the jacket.
- Practice at home in front of a mirror to see how little anyone will really see.
- Find a quiet place when you're out. You can nurse in your car for the most privacy if you are just not comfortable with nursing in public.
- Don't feel as if you have to hide in the bathroom to nurse your baby. Do it if you're comfortable with it, but if you'd rather not sit in a restroom nursing you can find a quiet place somewhere in most stores.
- Find out how the laws protect you in your state. Many (but not all) states have laws that protect a breastfeeding mom's right to nurse in public. In those states, anywhere that mom can legally be (like a store or restaurant) she can nurse her baby in peace, which means that people cannot ask her to leave or go to the restroom to nurse. If you know how you are protected in your state, then you'll feel more confident in your right to nurse anywhere.

Breastfeeding is painful and difficult.

Breastfeeding, when done correctly, is completely painless. Yes, you may be sore to begin with as you learn to latch baby on correctly, and you may encounter a few painful problems. For many of us there is a learning curve to nursing. Some women glide right through with no problems at all. Some women have every problem in the book. Other women fall somewhere in between. But once they get the hang of it, most moms find that breastfeeding is a breeze—painless and easy. If you find you are having trouble, don't give up. Seek help from a qualified lactation consultant or La Leche League leader.

Most of the benefits of breastfeeding happen during the first three months.

You may hear this from some physicians. But the fact is that you and baby reap the many immediate and long-term benefits of breastfeeding for as long as you do it. The risks of future diseases for your baby and you continue to decrease the longer you nurse.

You should only nurse your baby for 20 minutes at a time. Ten minutes on one side, then ten minutes on the other side.

While this is great advice for moms of babies who are efficient nursers, it doesn't work for everyone. Some babies are pretty laid back when it comes to nursing. They'll suck a little, rest, suck, and rest. These little ones are in no hurry. If you were to follow this guideline, you'd have one hungry little guy all the time! Nurse your baby for as long as he's nursing (actually drinking milk), and when you realize he's just hanging out, if you want you can take him off. Or leave him there if you're both happy.

Overcoming Obstacles

Some women fall into nursing very naturally and do not experience any problems at all. But for others an occasional problem will arise, and you should know what to look for in case you are experiencing pain or difficulty when you nurse.

Finding Support

Two of the biggest obstacles to breastfeeding are not having enough information and not getting sufficient support from the people around you, including your doctors. To have a successful breastfeeding relationship it is a tremendous help to have the support of your spouse or partner, your family and friends, and your doctor. If you are someone who ends up having problems here and there, you'll need to have people around you who will help you work through the problems and cheer you on as you continue to breastfeed your baby. It can be difficult to continue if people suggest to you at every minor setback that you just switch to formula. Support is essential to breastfeeding success.

To create your own support group amongst your family and friends, talk to them about breastfeeding. Read books on the topic and inform your circle of support about the benefits of breastfeeding and the risks of formula. Tell them how important it is to you to do this for your child and ask them to support you in that goal.

A Note from Jen about Breastfeeding and Doctors

I had problems with nursing my first baby. In fact, I had almost every problem you can have: thrush, plugged ducts, thrush, mastitis, thrush, an abscess that had to be surgically drained, and thrush. And did I mention the thrush? I actually had thrush (a yeast infection that gets passed back and forth between baby and mom) almost constantly for the first four and a half months of my son's life, with only about a week of painless nursing during that time. So when I talked to my pediatrician at the four-month check up, she suggested I start supplementing with formula, telling me that most of the good of breastfeeding happens during the first three months, and I had done that already.

Unfortunately, she gave me false information. Breastfeeding does do a lot of good for as long as you do it, and in some cases it offers better protection the longer you do it. But I didn't realize that at the time. I didn't know then what I know now (which is everything you're reading in this chapter), and regrettably I followed my doctor's advice. I started supplementing with formula when my son was four and a half months old, and he was completely weaned from the breast at six months. I did not intend to wean him, but my production went down so much with the supplementing, that it just happened, which made me so sad.

No offense to Jamie, but doctors, although they know a lot about many things, are sometimes not the best source of information for breastfeeding advice. (To be fair to Jamie, he is an exception, partly because of his personal interest and partly because his wife Caitlin has nursed four children for a cumulative time of nine and a half years). Most doctors, however, know very little about breastfeeding. It is not something that they usually learn in medical school, so unless they have a special interest in it, they are unlikely to have educated themselves about breastfeeding. If you find that you are having problems with breastfeeding, it is more than worth it to get another opinion (or two or three) from a trained lactation consultant or La Leche League leader. Do what you have to do to find the information and support you need to continue nursing.

The best people to talk to when you have a breastfeeding problem are lactation consultants. You can find them through your hospital, doctor's office, or the local chapter of La Leche League. They are trained in diagnosing and treating breastfeeding issues and are a great help to moms who are experiencing difficulties. For more information on breastfeeding support, see the Resources section at the end of this book.

How to Increase Your Milk Supply

- **Nurse. Nurse. Then nurse some more. Do it as often as possible.**
- **Pump after baby is done nursing or when he's taking a long nap.**
- **Fully drain the breast when nursing or pumping.**

Low Milk Production

If you seem to not be producing enough milk, your doctor may simply suggest supplementing with formula. This is not the best first step to take in most cases. Usually the best solution is to increase your milk production by nursing your baby as often as possible. Your baby stimulates milk production by nursing at your breast. The more you do it, the more milk you will produce. It's supply and demand: Your body will supply as much milk as your baby demands. (As we've mentioned, only rarely is a woman's milk production consistently insufficient for her baby.) If you supplement with formula right away, your baby will not be stimulating your production as much, and you will continue to not produce as much milk.

However, there are definitely times when supplements are necessary. If baby is failing to thrive, is dehydrated, or decidedly underfed, you will need to follow your doctor's advice to supplement with donor breast milk or formula. During this time you can try to keep your milk production up by pumping as often as possible, although pumps are not as effective as your baby at increasing your milk production.

Low Milk Supply May Be Due To:
- **Not nursing or pumping often enough**
- **Baby not being able to suck properly**
- **Mom not eating enough**
- **Rarely, mom might have a thyroid problem**

Tongue-Tied/Short Frenulum

If your baby has a tight frenulum (the tissue that connects the tongue to the floor of the mouth), it may cause pain with nursing. If your baby cannot stick his tongue out very far, or if the tongue indents into the shape of a heart when protruding, he may have a tight frenulum, also known as being "tongue-tied." If it isn't causing any nursing problems, there is no reason to "fix" it. But if you have an unusual amount of soreness with nursing, and seem to be getting a good latch, the short frenulum may be to blame.

The solution is simple. Your physician can quickly clip your baby's frenulum during an office visit. The physician simply lifts the tongue with one finger and snips the frenulum with small scissors. It rarely bleeds, and it doesn't seem to hurt. Most moms notice a reduction in their nursing pain immediately.

You many have to search for a physician willing to snip a frenulum. Many doctors are not trained in this procedure and are unwilling to do it. They may even tell you it is unnecessary. Good studies do show a benefit, however, and Jamie has had great success with this simple procedure. (So has Jen as a nursing mom.)

Bad Suck

Occasionally a baby may have trouble sucking, which can cause soreness for you. Take a look at your nipple after it comes out of baby's mouth. If the shape does not resemble what it looked like before it went into your baby's mouth, then a bad suck might be the problem. Contact a lactation consultant for help with retraining baby to suck properly.

Thrush

Thrush is a yeast infection that gets passed back and forth between baby and mom. If you are not experiencing any pain and your baby does not seem to be bothered, then no treatment is needed. However, thrush often causes serious pain for mom. Some women have described the pain to be burning or as if crushed glass were being ground into your nipples. You can get shooting pains in your breasts or back if the yeast gets into the milk ducts. The nipples may also be itchy or look shiny and pink.

Your baby may have white spots in his mouth or the appearance of spilled milk on the insides of his lips. He may be gassy and grumpy, and he might have a persistent diaper rash made up of little red bumps that won't go away with the use of diaper rash cream.

If you are in pain or your baby is uncomfortable, go see your doctor. Even if you are the only one being bothered (and even if you do not see signs of thrush in your baby's mouth or a yeast rash on his bottom), *both you and your baby need treatment*. If only you are treated, the thrush may get cleared up from your breasts, but baby will still have it and will re-infect you with it.

There are many things you can do to treat thrush. First, change your breast pads often so they remain dry. Do not wear the same nursing bra two days in a row, and wash your bras in hot water with vinegar added in the rinse. You can create a wash for your nipples of water and vinegar (1 cup of water with 1 tablespoon of vinegar), to swab on them after each feeding. Letting your nipples air dry helps too, because yeast loves to grow in warm, damp places (like moist breast pads).

Your doctor may prescribe Nystatin cream for your nipples and a Nystatin suspension for your baby. It has varying degrees of effectiveness. She may also be able to prescribe an all-purpose nipple ointment that has antifungal and antibiotic properties to help fight a yeast infection. (It can be used for cracked nipples or those that are just sore.)

You can also try an over-the-counter remedy of gentian violet (1% solution). It is a bright purple solution that you paint on your nipples or swab in baby's mouth (either way you do it, the point is to get the gentian violet on both your nipples and in baby's mouth by painting or swabbing, then nursing). One note of caution: Gentian violet will stain, so make sure you and baby are wearing clothes that you do not care about staining. (After you've nursed to share the gentian violet, you'll have a baby with purple all around his mouth, kind of like clown lips, though not as neat. You can easily get the purple off of skin by using natural, unscented baby wipes. Gently wipe baby's face until the purple is gone.) The gentian violet should be used for only seven days at a time.

If you have problems with recurring thrush, you may want to limit refined sugars and flours in your diet and think about ways to increase good bacteria in your body (either by eating more yogurt with live active cultures or taking probiotics).

Plugged Ducts

If your breasts have sore lumps in them, you probably have plugged milk ducts. The milk ducts are tubes that connect the milk production areas in the breast to the nipple. The best way to treat them is to nurse, nurse, and then nurse some more. Putting warm compresses on your breasts (or taking a hot shower) and massaging the plugged duct will also help to unplug it. Also try massaging your breast while nursing. (It hurts to massage plugged ducts, but it helps.) It is important to take care of plugged milk ducts as soon as you notice them. They are relatively easy to manage, but can give rise to mastitis if not properly cared for.

Mastitis

Mastitis is a breast infection. It occurs when a bacterial infection invades a plugged milk duct. If you have a plugged duct that becomes hard, with the skin on your breast becoming hot, swollen, and red, you very likely have mastitis.

The beginning treatment for mastitis is the same as for plugged ducts: nurse, nurse, and then nurse some more. If that doesn't work, call your doctor and find out what she recommends for treatment. You don't necessarily need to go on antibiotics right away. Antibiotics are often reserved for moms with accompanying fevers, who feel sicker and more achy (like the flu), or when the simple measures don't work in a few days. Remember to nurse your baby on both sides. Nursing on the side with the infection helps drain the duct and get rid of the infection, and continuing to breastfeed on the other side helps ensure that you won't create another plugged duct there,

> It is possible to have mastitis and not know it. If the infection is under the nipple, then you simply may not notice the nipple looking redder, darker, or swollen until it's too late. You may also not show other signs like fever and aches. It is, however, unmistakably painful. So if you are experiencing serious pain in your breast, see your doctor.

too. Surprisingly, there is no risk to the baby from nursing on the breast with the infection.

Still, you should get help right away to cure the infection to avoid an abscess if at all possible.

Breast Abscess

A breast abscess can develop when the bacterial infection of mastitis grows so rapidly that it turns the plugged milk duct into a pocket of pus. Though fortunately a rare occurrence, a breast abscess is very serious and requires medical attention. If your doctor has determined that you have an abscess, you'll need to find a surgeon to drain it. Make sure the surgeon you choose has experience draining breast abscesses.

After the abscess has been drained, you'll need to start nursing as soon as possible (or pumping if you're afraid nursing might hurt, depending on where the incision was). You want to make sure that breast keeps producing milk and also keep the other ducts clear while your breast is healing.

Teething

Some (not all) babies will start clamping down on your nipple when they start teething. It's uncomfortable, for sure, and it's something that you will want to teach him not to do. Tell him "Ow, that hurts!" as you pop him off your nipple. You want him to learn that when he bites, he stops nursing. As you learn to anticipate when he's about to clamp or pull (which you will!), you can quickly slide a finger into his mouth to unlatch him and remind him that he cannot bite you. Make sure you get that finger in between his upper and lower gums so he cannot bite down on your nipple as you start to pull it out of his mouth. That will save you some pain.

Does it hurt to nurse a baby who has teeth? No. It doesn't. The teeth are not used at all in nursing. In fact, the tongue covers the lower teeth while baby's breastfeeding, so it's actually impossible for him to bite you *while he's nursing.* But once he stops actually nursing . . . well, yes. Baby will sometimes bite you when he's teething. It's not personal, and he's not trying to hurt you. He's simply trying to relieve the pain he's feeling in his gums as those little teeth push through to the surface. That's why he chews on his hands and every toy that he gets hold of during this time. He's instinctively putting pressure on his very sore gums to help relieve the pain. You will just need to teach him that he cannot do that on your breasts.

Expressing Milk and Introducing Bottles

If you will be returning to work while your baby is still nursing, you will need to introduce a bottle. If you do it too early, it can cause problems with baby's latch when nursing. Though that kind of problem is fixable, it's best to avoid it. If at all possible, we recommend not using a pacifier or starting a bottle until the baby is nursing really well and gaining weight consistently, usually at around three to four weeks of life. This timing is important; if you wait too long to introduce it, like two to three months, baby may not take a bottle. You may also want to get baby used to having a bottle once in a while, even if you're going to be staying at home full time. That way someone else will be able to feed him too. It's also just fine if baby never has a bottle. Solely breastfeeding is perfectly fine, but it's more work for mom because she's the only source of food for the first six months until he starts solids.

The best time to introduce a bottle is around four to six weeks of age. Offer a bottle of expressed breast milk every other day or every couple of days at first, just to get baby used to the idea. If baby balks at taking a bottle, try different brands of bottles and nipples. It may just be that he doesn't like the shape or feel of the one you've given him, or you may need to have someone else offer the bottle to him. This is great for dads, partners, or grandparents. Baby may not want a bottle when he's leaning against the breast that feeds him, but he may be happy to take it from someone who doesn't have those breasts.

If you will be going back to work, you will probably want to invest in an electric pump. It is the most efficient way of expressing breast milk. Ask friends, family, and lactation consultants to get recommendations. It is sometimes possible to rent a pump for as little as a dollar a day to "test drive" it. If you will be staying home, you can use either an electric or a manual pump, depending on how often you plan to pump or just based on personal preference.

Storing Breast Milk

Fresh breast milk that you've just pumped will keep at room temperature for close to ten hours. But if you are home, it's best to refrigerate or freeze the milk as soon as you've pumped it. Breast milk will keep in the refrigerator for five days and in the freezer for three months. Always be sure to label containers with the date you pumped the milk so you can use the oldest milk first and will know if some milk has been in the freezer or refrigerator for too long. Never refreeze milk that you've defrosted. If you've defrosted too much, throw out the leftover milk.

The best way to defrost frozen breast milk is by placing the bag or bottle in a bowl of warm water. When the water cools, pour it out and replace it with a fresh supply of warm water. Do that until the milk is completely thawed and feels a little warm. Shake it to redistribute the fat, and then pour it into a clean bottle for baby to drink from. Do not microwave breast milk or heat it on the stove. Getting the breast milk too hot can cause a loss of vitamin C, and can also destroy some of its antibodies. Microwaving can create hot spots in the milk that can burn baby's mouth, and if you microwave milk stored in plastic containers, the plastic can filter into the milk and be ingested by baby as he eats.

To Pacify or Not to Pacify

The decision to use pacifiers is completely personal. They are a wonderful comfort to some babies and children, and they offer the nursing mom a break when baby simply needs to suck but doesn't need sustenance. They can be used to help a child relax into sleep or to comfort a baby during a long car ride. They can also be a tremendous source of comfort when baby is teething. Additionally, the AAP has found that the use of pacifiers might reduce the risk of SIDS.

There are a few drawbacks to pacifiers, though. First and most important, your baby will likely become very attached to the pacifier, which will make it difficult to wean him from it. Depending on when and how you do it, this can be very stressful for him, comparable to taking away a beloved blanket or stuffed animal. Generally, the older the child is, the easier it will be to help him give it up. Try to look at it from your child's point of view and base your timing on whether your child is really ready for this change. Do your best to wean with understanding and gentleness.

Probably the most annoying thing about using pacifiers is having to keep track of them. You may have to find a pacifier in the middle of the night when it has fallen out of your baby's mouth and he needs it to fall asleep again. Once he's mobile and motoring around with pacifiers, he'll leave them all over the house. So will you. Finding one when you need one may not be easy when they've been distributed among the house, cars, and diaper bag.

If you decide to use a pacifier, it's best to wait until your baby is at least three to four weeks old before introducing it. That way he's less likely to have trouble with his latch, as he will be an expert at breastfeeding by then. In some cases, babies just will not take a pacifier and will settle for nothing less than the real thing—mama's soft, warm, comfy breast. That's okay. Follow your baby's lead.

Breastfeeding your baby is an incredible experience that benefits you and your baby in so many amazing ways. It can be difficult at first for some moms—sometimes the first month can be quite a challenge, to say the least. But if you can get through that, you are in for some wonderful experiences with your baby. We wish you great success in your breastfeeding relationship with your baby!

Feeding Your Baby

12

Your mom said it best—you are what you eat. The same goes for your baby. So if you want a healthy baby, you need to feed her well. Start with a wide variety of good quality, colorful foods, for both you and your baby. Listen to your body (and let your baby listen to hers) to avoid overeating. And model healthy eating habits for your child. With childhood obesity and diabetes rates increasing, it's prudent to establish healthy eating habits right from the start.

Introducing solid foods can be fun—and messy. It's a huge developmental step for your baby. At first, the purpose of feeding her solids is to develop her palate, but over time, she will eventually grow into eating food for nutrition. As she nears her first birthday, solid foods will begin to provide her better nutrition than breast milk or formula (though breast milk can continue to be an excellent supplement).

We recommend a relaxed approach to feeding a baby. If you are worried about how much or how little your baby is eating, know that each child is going to eat as much or as little as it takes to fill her tummy, so follow baby's lead on how much she eats. There are only a few rules to introducing solids, and there is a huge list of great foods to start her on during the second half of her first year.

Formula Feeding

Occasionally breastfeeding doesn't work out for some women and that's okay. That's what formula is for. Although breast milk is the preferred food, babies raised on formula can do just fine. (See Chapter Eleven for more information on breastfeeding.)

If you will be feeding your baby formula, ask your pediatrician what formula she recommends. As a general rule, all formulas have similar nutritional content and most babies will tolerate them. The newest formulas, many with highly advertised nutrient additives, are more expensive but have not been shown to provide any significant additional benefit to your baby. We suggest you save your money and buy the most basic, inexpensive formula for your child. If that is not well tolerated for some reason (such as gas or poor weight gain), you can always try a different brand.

Formula comes in three forms: powder, concentrated liquid, and ready-to-serve. (We've listed them in order of expense, from least to most.) You must add water to both the powder and the concentrated liquid formulas. The form you use is up to you—one is usually not better than another. Most formulas are already iron enriched, so try low-iron formulas if your child seems to be having issues such as constipation that might be related to the iron.

When choosing which type of bottle or nipple to use, we again suggest that you save your money and buy the most basic, inexpensive kind to start. Most babies do fine with standard bottles and nipples. If your baby seems to be having problems with gas, some parents

Buying and Using Formula Safely

Always check the expiration date on cans of formula before you buy them, and again before you feed the formula to your baby. *Never* feed your baby expired formula.

recommend angled bottles, which have a slight angle to them midway down the bottle. This angle helps keep the air inside the bottle farther away from the nipple, which means your baby will take in less air and have less gas. Another option is to try bottles that use sterilized bags to hold the breast milk or formula. You can actually squeeze out all the air from the bag before feeding your baby, therefore virtually eliminating the possibility of her swallowing air, even if she finishes every single drop. Along the same lines, some parents recommend special nipples that lessen air intake for gassy babies. And you may find that your baby prefers one type of nipple over another! However, it's best to wait and see if you'll need these special items before you buy them.

When using bottles to feed your baby (whether breast milk or formula), you need to insure that the bottles and nipples are clean. The average dishwasher will get your supplies clean. If you do not have a dishwasher, or if you are worried that yours does not get your bottles and nipples clean enough, wash them in hot soapy water using a bottle brush. Some parents sterilize the bottles and nipples weekly (or even before each use!) by boiling them in an open pan of water for five minutes. If you are using bottle bags, you can skip this extra step for the bottles, because the bags come sterile and ready to fill.

If you will be mixing powdered or concentrated formula, and you live in an older house (which may have lead pipes), consider testing your water for lead. If you use well water, test to make sure the coliform count is below the recommended threshold. (You might want to do this test on a yearly basis.) Also, there is an ongoing debate as to whether you need to use sterile water when mixing formula. If you opt for sterile water, you can make your tap or bottled water sterile by bringing it to a boil and then letting it cool to be ready for use. But many experts feel that there are no safety concerns with using regular tap water for mixing formula. The only exception to this is using tap water when the community has a public health advisory regarding the water. In those circumstances, it will be very well advertised that you should not use the tap water for infant feeding.

How much formula should your baby be taking every day? As much as she wants. Children regulate their food intake quite well, eating when they are hungry and stopping when they are full. Your job is to offer enough food to satisfy her without encouraging her to overeat. If you find that she is no longer interested in eating but is just playing with the bottle and gazing around the room at more interesting objects, then she is probably done for the time being.

We realize that this answer might not satisfy all parents, but it is true. The actual volume of formula intake is less important than how she is following the growth curves over time. Remember that some babies will be seventeen pounds on their first birthday while others will be twenty-seven pounds—and they both may be perfectly healthy!

On a practical note, however, you should probably have one more ounce of formula in each bottle than what your baby normally eats. So if she usually takes three to four ounces at a feeding, you would want to have five ounces in each bottle in case she is extra hungry.

Hold Your Baby!
Feeding your baby is the perfect time to really connect with her, so we encourage you to hold your baby in your arms for feedings rather than letting her feed on her own. You'll create a lasting bond with your beautiful little person.

If you will be using formula throughout the day, consider mixing a larger amount in a big container all at once. Keep the container in the fridge, filling bottles as you need them. Discard whatever your baby does not eat at each feeding; do not put the partially full bottle back in the fridge for baby to finish later (there is a risk that bacteria could build up and contaminate the formula). Use the mixed formula within twenty-four hours or discard any leftovers after that time and make a fresh batch. If you will be going out of the house, you can mix bottles in advance and take them with you. Just remember to keep them cool so they don't spoil. Alternatively, you can take empty bottles and little containers or baggies of pre-measured formula. When baby is hungry, pour the required amount of water in the bottle, add the pre-measured formula, and mix.

You can use bottles right out of the refrigerator or choose to warm them up. A breastfed baby is more likely to want warm milk because that's what she's used to getting from her mother's breast. A formula-fed baby doesn't need the formula warmed, unless he's used to taking it that way. If you do warm up a bottle, *do not* heat it in a microwave. Uneven heating

> **Making Formula**
> Follow the mixing directions on the can of formula. Do not dilute the mixture (add too much water) or make it more concentrated (add too little water). Both can have harmful effects on your baby. Follow the directions given exactly.

of the liquid can make some of the formula too hot and burn baby when she drinks it. It is much safer to use a bottle warmer, if you have one, or to warm the bottle the old-fashioned way, in a bowl of warm water. Keep replacing the water in the bowl as it cools until the liquid in the bottle is the desired temperature. Test the temperature first, before giving it to your baby. Place a few drops on the inside of your wrist to feel whether the liquid is warm enough or too hot. If it is too hot, place the bottle in a bowl of cool water to cool it down.

Be sure to burp your baby after feeding her a bottle of breast milk or formula. Babies can take more air into their tummies than necessary when they drink from a bottle, which can be painful if you do not help move it back out of their bodies. You will want to make sure baby is upright and you are putting pressure on her tummy to help move the air up and out.

Introducing Solids

It is best to wait until your baby is about six months old (or older) before introducing solid foods. Feeding your baby solid foods before this age can increase her risk of developing food sensitivities or allergies. So, while it is exciting to start feeding your baby food, please wait until she's old enough and showing signs that she's ready.

How will you know when she's ready? She'll tell you in several ways. First, she will become more and more interested in what you're doing when you're eating. She will reach for your food, and she will carefully watch each bite as it leaves the plate and travels to your mouth. In addition to her interest in food, she should be able to sit up relatively well. She doesn't have to be able to completely sit on her own, but she should be able to hold herself upright in a high chair (as opposed to sliding down to a slouch). She should also have pretty good hand-eye coordination and be able to get things into her mouth fairly well on her own. Finally, she should not push the food back out at you with her tongue but rather be able to use her tongue to swallow it.

Once you've determined that your baby is ready for food, prepare yourself. Babies are messy creatures. As your baby is learning how to get the food from the table or tray into her mouth, she'll also be discovering the joys of gravity as she watches pea after pea after pea fall to the floor. She'll enjoy the feeling of squishing food through her fingers or "painting" with food as she spreads it all over her tray or the table or her face. It's a messy affair! But it's also very normal behavior.

Try not to stress about how messy your baby or the floor or the table (or the dog) gets during the meal. Just go with the flow and clean up after it's all done. You'll drive yourself crazy (and your baby, too, for that matter) if you spend the entire time trying to keep her neat and clean. Let her explore and learn, and save the cleaning up for when she's done.

A word about gravity: It's the law. No, seriously, babies dropping things to the floor is developmentally appropriate. Even though it may not be a behavior that you want to encourage, try to remember that they are little scientists discovering how the world works. Offer her an alternative to dropping food. Ask your baby not to drop food but to try dropping a toy instead. If she still continues to drop food, she is probably no longer interested in eating, so feel free to consider mealtime over. She can still test the laws of gravity after she is cleaned up and back to playing with toys.

You can also be proactive to make after-meal cleanup easier and quicker. Place a tarp, old sheet, picnic table cloth, or something similar under your baby's high chair to catch any spills and keep them off the carpet. If you have wood or linoleum floors, you don't need the tarp, but you may choose to use one anyway. Also, find bibs that have a pocket to catch food and are easy to clean by either wiping them down or rinsing them off in the sink. That way your baby's clothes will be less likely to get stained. And, by the way, baby food does stain! Carrots will turn your baby's clothes orange.

Begin with just one feeding a day. On the first day, choose only one kind of food to feed him for his meal. Then you can add more foods as you go along. Some books suggest waiting three or even seven days before adding the next food, but we feel that is unnecessary. You can add new foods daily if that feels right to you.

When you think your baby might want to eat another meal during the day (it doesn't matter whether it's a few weeks after starting with one meal or a couple of months later), add another meal into your daily schedule. Have baby eat when you eat, if possible. Start a family tradition of sitting down together for meals from the very beginning. After you feed solids to your baby, nurse her or give her formula. She still needs it.

First Food Rules

1. Choose soft, mushy foods. (For starters, you can try ripe bananas, mashed potatoes, avocado, applesauce, cooked

sweet potato, and baby cereal mixed with breast milk, formula, or water.)

2. Introduce only one new food per day at most. (You can feed one new food *in addition to* the foods baby has already tried.) Or you can wait a few days in between new foods. You decide.

3. Until baby is one year old, avoid honey and cow's milk.

4. If you have a family history of food allergies, consider delaying possible allergy-causing foods until your baby is more than a year old. Common foods that are associated with allergies are nuts, dairy products, wheat, seafood, and egg whites.

Now that you are ready and your baby is ready, what should you feed her first? In truth, there isn't one perfect first food—there are many great choices to select from. Soft, mushy food is a *must* at the beginning because firmer food is a choking hazard, so choose from these foods first. Good choices include ripe bananas, avocado, mashed potato, cooked sweet potato, applesauce, and baby cereal mixed with breast milk, formula, or water. Honey and cow's milk, however, should be avoided until after baby's first birthday.

Solids Are Supplements

Remember that solid food during the first year is only supplementary to breast milk or formula. Baby will still get most of her nutrition from breast milk or formula, so do not cut back on what you're already giving her when you start to introduce solid foods.

You can try one new food a day to see how your baby reacts. If she likes it, keep giving it to her. If she doesn't like it, try it again in a week or so. Offer her that particular food every so often to see if she develops a taste for it. If she appears to have a mild allergic reaction to a food (a few scattered swollen skin patches with itching but no breathing or swallowing problems), stop giving it to her and try it again in a few months. If she has the same reaction the second time you give it to her, then leave it out of her diet, and ask your doctor for advice on when you might try it again. Some children will outgrow food allergies, but it may take a couple of years. (If your baby has a *serious* allergic reaction, such as hives or problems breathing, the first time she tries a new food, *do not* feed it to her a second time. Allergic reactions can be worse for each subsequent exposure. Talk to your doctor about it.)

If you think your baby is ready for solids, but after a few tries you find that she doesn't seem that interested in solid foods after all, then close up shop and try again in a few days, weeks, or next month, whenever she starts to show signs again that she's interested. Don't sweat it; she'll be eating soon enough.

As your baby gets used to the action of taking food into her mouth and swallowing, you'll be able to give her foods that have more form. Give her plenty of time to adjust and learn this new skill. And feed her a variety of foods! Make them colorful! The actual purpose of giving your baby solid food during her first year of life is to expose her to many different flavors and broaden her palate. So there is no reason to limit baby to bland food. Let baby eat what you are eating. Just make sure that what you give her is not a choking hazard. Put it in a blender if you need to or cut it into small, *soft* pieces. If your baby becomes accustomed to a wide variety of different flavors and textures, she is more likely to eat a good mix of healthy foods when she is older.

By the way, healthy eating while you are breastfeeding is your baby's first taste of different foods. What you eat flavors your milk, so if you eat a wide variety of healthy foods, then you are beginning the process of broadening your baby's palate even before she tries solids.

An Alternative Way to Feed

Some parents encourage self-feeding from the start, and rarely, if ever, spoon-feed their baby. When their baby is developmentally ready, they offer whole soft foods, like banana or avocado, for baby to hold in her hand and take bites from when she's ready. These parents have found that their baby gags less often because she's taking bites that are an appropriate size for her mouth rather than putting a whole piece of food in her mouth that was cut up for her and may be too large.

Many parents have had great success with this method, serving baby only foods that she can pick up on her own. Some firmer foods like apples work well with this method, too. Baby can hold a peeled apple in her hands and scrape off tiny pieces with her front teeth, enjoying the small apple bits and the juice she gets. Babies tend to be ready for this type of feeding closer to eight months old, rather than at six months.

Establishing Healthy Eating

Here is our best advice for giving your baby a healthy diet:

1. Delay introducing sugary foods for as long as possible. Yes, she will eventually eat candy, but you don't have to get her hooked on it as a toddler.
2. Choose whole wheat and whole grain breads and crackers.
3. Use whole foods over processed foods as much as possible. (Whole foods are foods as nature intended, for the most part. They are single items—no list of ingredients to them, just the foods as they are naturally. Examples include fruits, vegetables, grains such as rice, oats, and coarse-ground wheat. Processed foods include refined flours, sugars, cookies, candy, and any packaged food high in fat, sugar, and salt.)
4. Avoid hydrogenated or partially-hydrogenated fats (trans fats). These fats are in many packaged, processed foods. Check the ingredients list for the terms "hydrogenated" or "partially-hydrogenated," even if the package says "0g Trans Fats," because small amounts may still be in the food.

5. Offer a wide variety of colorful fruits and vegetables.

6. Introduce water (it will take some time for baby to get used to the taste of water, but she will eventually if you keep giving it to her). As baby nears her first birthday, when she starts drinking something other than breast milk or formula, encourage her to drink water.

7. If you give your baby juice, choose only 100 percent juice. (Many juice drinks contain only a little actual juice and a lot of high-fructose corn syrup and water.) Dilute juices with water and limit intake to one bottle or cup per day.

8. Let your baby stop eating when she wants to. Do not encourage her to eat more—to finish her plate or bottle or the last two spoonfuls from the jar—when she indicates that she is finished. Allow her to listen to her body and stop eating when it tells her it's full. This is a good healthy eating habit for her to learn right from the beginning.

These are actually good eating tips for people of all ages—babies, children, and adults. Your child is going to eat whatever you eat, so if you want your child to eat in a healthy manner, then you must eat in a healthy manner as well. She will follow your example and will eat the foods you enjoy and have around. She will not be deprived if you do not give her lollypops or candy bars.

See the section on page 168 for a list of great foods to give your baby from six months on. (Note: You may see infant feeding charts that break down when to introduce certain foods to baby by month. These charts are just guides, not hard-and-fast rules for the order in which to introduce certain foods. We are simply offering you a list of healthy foods to give your baby, and you can choose when you want to introduce what.) The following list of suggested foods is by no means complete. Feed your baby the same healthy foods you are eating (except for honey and cow's milk if your baby is under twelve months).

Foods for Baby's First Year

Fruits

Banana (ripe)	Avocado
Apricot	Nectarine
Peach	Pears
Plums	Applesauce
Prunes	Mango
Papaya	Cantaloupe
Watermelon	Tomatoes
Pineapple	Kiwi
Berries (cut into small pieces)	

Vegetables

Sweet potato	Potatoes (mashed)
Squash (butternut, acorn, etc.)	Asparagus
Broccoli	Cauliflower
Spinach	Kale
Carrots	Green beans
Legumes (lentils, black beans, etc.)	Peas
Brussels sprout	Beets
Eggplant	Rutabaga
Turnips	Onion

Protein/dairy*

Whole-milk yogurt	Cottage cheese
Real cheese (not "processed cheese food")	Egg yolk (whole egg at one year)
Lean meats	Fish
Tofu	

Whole grain cereals

Oatmeal	Millet
Brown rice	Barley

Other grains

O-shaped cereals

Teething biscuits

Pasta

Pancakes

Whole grain crackers

Whole wheat/grain toast

Wheat bagels

Remember . . .

- First foods should be soft and mushy, whether whole (like a ripe banana), mashed, or pureed (like applesauce). Steam, microwave, roast, or boil hard vegetables and fruits to soften them.
- Once baby has mastered the soft mushy food, she can move up to finger foods—those that are still soft enough to disintegrate in the mouth, but that can be picked up by baby.
- You can also feed your baby what you are eating, as long as it is not a choking hazard.

*While you should avoid cow's milk until your baby is a year old (because it can interfere with iron absorption), you don't need to avoid all dairy products such as cheese or yogurt. Having said that, some families choose to delay all dairy products until after the first year of life.

Make It Yourself!

It is incredibly easy to make your own baby food, and it saves money. You can make your own pureed baby food, just like the stuff you can buy in the jars. What you create at home actually tastes so much better than what's in baby food jars! It's more flavorful because there are no added ingredients or preservatives, and it tastes fresh. But don't forget that your baby can eat whatever you are eating at the time (as long as it's safe), so you may not need to make a special baby food for her on every occasion.

Here is the whole process: Cook the food. Bake or steam a sweet potato, for example. Then place it in a blender or food processor. Add some water and blend until smooth. Fill ice cube trays with the puree, cover with foil, and place in the freezer. Once the cubes are frozen, empty the trays into zip-top freezer bags, and voila! You have baby food. How simple is that?! When you want to serve some to your baby, simply defrost a cube or two. (See below for tips on warming baby food.) You may need to add a little water to make the consistency runnier if you are just starting to introduce solids to your baby.

You can make your own baby cereal by grinding whole grains in a blender or food processor until they resemble flour. It usually takes about two minutes on high, and you should not blend more than one-half cup at a time to make sure it is all ground well. Make a lot, and keep it in canning jars in the fridge. When you want to cook some, boil one cup of water, sprinkle about three table-spoons of ground grains into the boiling water and whisk until smooth. Cook for about ten minutes on low heat, stirring con-stantly. If the cereal is too thick, add breast milk, formula, or water. If it's too thin, add wheat germ or store-bought baby cereal to get the consistency you want.

Have fun feeding your baby! Give her lots of fresh food and a great variety of it so she will be primed for a lifetime of healthy eating. Eat healthy yourself, and she will follow your example. Bon appétit!

Warming Baby Food

Always test how hot a food is before you give it to your baby. The best way to see if a food is the right temperature is to put some on a spoon and touch the food to your lips. If it feels hot on your lips, let it cool a bit before feeding it to your baby. Test it again after you've let it cool, and once more before you put it in your baby's mouth.

If you use a microwave, use 50 percent power and be sure to completely mix the food after heating to avoid hot spots that could burn baby's mouth. Remember, never use a microwave to heat breast milk or a bottle.

If you do not have a microwave and you need to heat up frozen food cubes, place them either in a pan on the stove (don't let them get hot enough to completely melt) or place them in a bowl and put that bowl in a pan of warm water. The warm water will heat the bowl, which will in turn melt the food cubes. (You may have to replace the water a few times as it cools.) If you think of it ahead of time, you can also select some food cubes the night before, place them in a covered container or bowl in the fridge and let them thaw overnight.

13

Vaccinations

From a public health perspective the benefits of vaccines are monumental. In the 1940s, over 3 million cases of measles were reported in the United States, as opposed to only 37 reported cases in 2004, the lowest ever recorded. Similarly, polio, once feared for its crippling effects, has been almost eradicated from the globe. This reduction in preventable childhood diseases through the use of vaccines means not only fewer sick children, but also fewer hospitalizations and deaths as a result of those illnesses.

However, vaccines, like all medicines, have side effects. Most are mild, such as a sore arm or slight fever. But in rare cases, side effects can be severe. It used to be that nearly all families knew someone with the complications brought about by childhood illness, such as paralysis due to polio, so, naturally, parents were more worried about the disease than any risks the vaccines posed. Now, with the disease rates so low, many parents seem more worried about their babies' reactions to the vaccines. In addition, many parents worry about unknown side effects that have not yet appeared or been recognized.

It doesn't help that we don't like to see our children cry from shots. Nor does it help that some parents feel coerced by the requirements that our children must be vaccinated before attending day care or public school. The fact that there are so many vaccines to consider complicates the issue even further. As of 2007, the recommended vaccine schedule for children under two years old includes ten separate vaccines and a minimum of seventeen needles.

So what is a parent to do?

Vaccine Basics

First, what exactly is a vaccine? A vaccine is a preparation that contains a disease-producing organism (like a bacterium or a virus), or part of that organism, that when administered to a person, stimulates the body into producing antibodies, or protection, against the disease. Depending on the type, the vaccine will either be unable to spread the disease at all or will give a person just a very mild version of the illness.

The vaccine works because your baby's immune system recognizes the organism as a foreign object, and over one to two weeks makes antibodies to remove it from it his body. Those particular antibodies disappear over time, but the ability to make them resides in his immune memory. If the organism is ever encountered again, your baby's body will recognize it and can produce the antibodies again, but even faster, within one to two days. Thus, if he is ever exposed to the disease in the future, he won't get sick because his body can contain and eliminate the organism before it causes the illness.

It is not entirely clear why vaccines cause side effects. It may be that the body reacts poorly to the organism in the vaccine or possibly to the preservatives used in it. It also appears that the method of administering the vaccine plays a role as there are different side effects for injections as compared to orally or nasally administered vaccines.

Risk-Benefit Analysis of Vaccines

We want to be clear about one thing from the start. If you don't have any concerns, we recommend all the vaccines listed in this chapter. We feel that the benefits outweigh the risks, both for the individual and for society as a whole.

We recognize, however, that many parents have mixed feeling about vaccines. While some parents object to all vaccines on religious or philosophical grounds, other parents are concerned with only certain vaccines or certain side effects. These parents find themselves struggling with the decision of whether to vaccinate their children against certain diseases.

If you are hesitant about giving your child any of the recommended vaccines, ask yourself this question: If your family were traveling to a third-world country where you would be exposing your child to polio, measles, and other vaccine-preventable illnesses, would you consider vaccinating your child? If your answer is "yes," this implies that you are doing a risk-benefit analysis of the vaccine.

What do we mean by a risk-benefit analysis? It means that you are not opposed to vaccines in all situations, but that you consider them on a case-by-case basis. You are weighing the risks of the vaccine (known and unknown side effects) versus the benefits (minimized risk of contracting the disease). For

> **We feel it is important to consciously recognize this decision-making process as a risk-benefit analysis. This type of analysis removes some emotional overlay and helps you identify what factors you want to consider when deciding about certain vaccines. For most parents, it demonstrates that at least under certain circumstances they might decide to vaccinate their child.**

example, when considering vaccinations in the United States, where there is a low risk of contracting these diseases, you might decide the vaccine's benefits do not outweigh the risks. However, when traveling in a country where the risk of getting the illness is higher, you might decide that the benefits of the vaccines outweigh the risk of any side effects.

The Vaccines and the Diseases

Below you will find a list of vaccinations commonly given in the first year of life, along with an explanation of each. Those we highly recommend are listed first, followed by those that we consider less critical.

As we mentioned, if you don't have a strong feeling against vaccines, we recommend them all. Most physicians and public heath officials feel the benefits outweigh the risks, both for your family and as a society. On a personal note, Jamie has seen children die of vaccine-preventable diseases while working in Africa. These diseases are real, and they still exist in many parts of the world. While he strongly defends the right of parents to decline vaccinations, he also strongly recommends the vaccines at every well-child visit.

If you have questions or concerns about the vaccines, consider the following issues when making your own risk-benefit analysis:

1. How serious is the disease if my child gets it?
2. How likely is it that my child will get the disease?
3. How serious are the side effects associated with the vaccine?
4. How likely is it that my child will get the side effects?
5. How effective is the vaccine?

CDC Recommended Vaccine Schedule 2007

The most current schedule and relevant footnotes may be found at http://www.cdc.gov/nip/recs/child-schedule.htm.

Remember that this is the *recommended* schedule. It was chosen to maximize the public health benefits and to minimize the number of office visits and injections each child is given. You are free to work with your doctor to create an alternative schedule if it will make you feel more comfortable. One mom in Jamie's practice wanted to give only one vaccine at a time to her baby and preferred using as few combination vaccines as possible. In the end, instead of giving three injections at the two-, four-, and six-month well-child visits, she chose to come to the office at weekly intervals for fifteen separate visits over six months. The goal for you is to vaccinate your child in whatever way makes you feel most comfortable.

One last note: If your child is sick or has been sick within a few days before your scheduled doctor's appointment, discuss this with your physician before your child receives the vaccination. If your child has a mild illness, such as an ear infection, mild respiratory infection, or diarrhea, that is generally not enough to recommend against vaccinations. However, if your child is moderately or severely ill, you will want to delay getting the vaccines at that visit. And of course, if your child had a severe reaction to a previous vaccine, discuss that reaction with your doctor before a booster dose is given.

Haemophilus Influenza Type B (HIB)

The HIB vaccine is a very effective and safe vaccine. When looking at the risk-benefit analysis, first recognize that the risks of the disease are significant. *HIB meningitis* (inflammation of the lining of the spinal cord and brain) is a severe illness that can lead to death or prolonged neurological deficits like deafness. At the very least, the infection requires a ten- to fourteen-day hospital stay with antibiotics, IVs, and multiple spinal taps. HIB epiglottis (inflammation of the flap over the windpipe) creates swelling in the upper windpipe that leads to children choking on their own airways. Not only is that frightening, but it also requires intubation (inserting a tube down the windpipe) plus IVs and antibiotics for several days. No parent ever wants their child to experience either of these troubling diseases.

The benefits of the vaccine are clear. After the vaccine was introduced in the late 1980s, the rate of severe HIB disease dropped from twenty thousand to one hundred cases per year in just ten years. Despite this reduction in the severe disease, however, HIB bacteria are still prevalent in our society. Adults can have this illness and exhibit only mild symptoms such as conjunctivitis or bronchitis. But children under five, and especially those under two, have the potential to develop severe complications that will put them in the hospital. We can't assume that children will never be exposed to this disease.

The side effects of the vaccine are very mild, generally just a sore arm and low-grade fever, and only a minority of patients experience that. An Australian study linked the HIB vaccine with juvenile diabetes, but further studies have not been able to support that finding. Fortunately, there are no known severe reactions.

With all this in mind, the HIB vaccine is an excellent choice, especially for parents who are nervous about vaccines in general. The CDC's recommended schedule for the HIB vaccine is two, four, and six months with a booster at twelve to fifteen months, but this can vary slightly with the type of HIB vaccine used.

Pneumococcal vaccine

Infection with *Streptococcal pneumoniae* bacteria, otherwise known as pneumococcus, is similar to HIB in many ways. It causes severe illnesses such as meningitis, pneumonia, and bacterial infections in the bloodstream, but it also causes more than five million ear infections a year in children. Like HIB, the vaccine has decreased the incidence of serious infections. The bacteria are common in society, affecting adults as well as children.

The pneumococcal vaccine was introduced in the last ten years, so it has not yet caused as dramatic a reduction in related diseases as the HIB vaccine. In addition, it has more side effects, the most common of which is fever—both more fevers in general and higher fevers overall (over 102 degrees Fahrenheit). Fortunately, it has not yet been shown to cause any serious, irreversible side effects. It is also recommended to be given at two, four, and six months, with a booster at twelve to fifteen months.

Diphtheria, Tetanus, and acellular Pertussis (DTaP)

This combination vaccine protects against three diseases. *Diphtheria* is very rare in the United States, but it is certainly still possible (as described above in the case of the former Soviet Union). *Tetanus* is caused by bacteria found in the soil and causes lockjaw. It is one of the few vaccine-preventable illnesses that's not contagious, meaning that one person can't get it from another. What is relevant about tetanus is that kids can be exposed to it when playing outdoors.

Pertussis, also known as whooping cough, is the only vaccine-preventable illness that has been *increasing* in incidence over the last ten years. In 2003, there were more than eleven thousand cases reported in the United States. Unfortunately, even if you have received the vaccine or actually had the disease, protection against this illness wanes over time. So adolescents and adults can get the disease even after having received the vaccine or having contracted the illness and could develop a lingering cough. That's not so bad. However, if they spread the disease to infants, it can lead to severe coughing spells that might prevent a baby from eating, drinking, or even breathing. Such spells can lead to hospitalization and even death.

The DTaP vaccine is associated with rare side effects such as nonstop crying for over three hours (one in one thousand), seizures (one in fourteen thousand), high fevers over 105 degrees Fahrenheit (one in sixteen thousand), and possible permanent brain damage (unclear but estimated at one in one million). These estimates are from the CDC but other organizations suggest that the risks are higher.

Naturally parents are worried about these potential side effects. When faced with the decision, you have to weigh the real risks of the disease versus the real risks of the vaccines. In our opinion, given the continued and increasing presence of the illness, the vaccine is a good choice. It is recommended to be given at two, four, and six months, with a booster at fifteen to eighteen months and four to six years. A variation of the DTaP called Tdap is recommended as a booster for adolescents and adults.

Influenza

The influenza vaccine protects against the influenza virus which causes fevers, coughs, fatigue, and muscle aches. What most people call the "flu" is usually just a mild cold, but true influenza usually has a person lying in bed for a few days with a high fever and terrible body aches. For healthy adults, the illness is inconvenient, but for certain members of the population, including children under five years old, it can lead to more severe problems. In the United States, millions of people are infected annually; an estimated two hundred thousand people are hospitalized, and thirty-six thousand die each year from complications of influenza. While most of these hospitalizations and deaths occur in adults, some of them do occur in children.

The vaccine usually has only mild side effects such as a sore arm. There were several cases of Guillian-Barre syndrome (a temporary neuromuscular problem) in the 1970s associated with a certain type of influenza vaccine, but more recent vaccines do not appear to have that risk. Given the pervasiveness of the illness and the mildness of the side effects, we recommend the influenza vaccine.

The CDC recommends that the vaccine be given between October and March of each year for children ages six months to five years, preferably in October or November so the child is well protected before the winter flu season. It is recommended that in the first season the vaccine is given, a booster follows one month later. Some versions of the vaccine contain trace amounts of thimerosal, or mercury, while others are thimerosal-free. The CDC does not consider the trace amount significant, but if this is important to you, be sure to insist upon the mercury-free version.

Hepatitis B

As discussed in Chapter Three, hepatitis B is a virus that affects the liver and is transmitted by direct contact with blood (through blood transfusions, IV drug use, or sexual intercourse, for example). Even though most children are not at risk for these behaviors until the teenage years, younger children are sometimes infected by chance exposure to someone else's blood, such as toddler injuries in a day care setting. If a person is infected, there is the risk that he will become a chronic carrier of the virus, meaning that he will have it for the rest of his life and can spread it to others. In addition, chronic carriers also have a much higher risk of liver illnesses, liver failure, and even liver cancer.

Fortunately, the vaccine is very protective and very safe with only mild side effects, generally a sore arm and mild fevers. There are a number of recommended schedules; a common one is to give the vaccine at birth, then at two, four, and six months of age. This vaccine is often found in combination with other vaccines, which allows you to minimize the number of needles your child will receive.

Polio (IPV)

Polio was once a dreaded illness that caused thousands of cases of paralysis in the United States in the early 1900s. Fortunately, due to a worldwide vaccination campaign, polio has become increasingly rare, with only twelve hundred reported cases in the world in 2004. The Western Hemisphere, which includes the United States, was certified free of wild polio virus in 1994, meaning that the only reported cases that occurred at that point were due to the oral polio vaccine.

The recommended vaccine used in the United States is an injection given at two and four months, with a booster between six and eighteen months, and another booster between the ages of four and six years. (The oral vaccine that you might remember from your childhood has not been used since 2000 because in rare instances it could cause the actual disease.) The side effects of the vaccine are minimal (usually just a sore arm), and no serious side effect has ever been documented. The polio vaccine can be given alone or in combination with other recommended vaccines.

Rotavirus

Rotavirus is a virus that causes diarrhea. Almost every infant will get one rotavirus illness in the first year of life, and thus there will be millions of infections in the United States every year. Of those, about fifty thousand infants will be hospitalized.

The recommended vaccine is given orally at two, four, and six months of age. Studies show that use of the vaccine decreases emergency room visits and hospitalizations by around 95 percent. The potential side effects are minimal, with 3 percent of children developing some diarrhea or vomiting in the first week after the vaccine. No serious side effects have been noted. However, as discussed above, a previous version of this vaccine was associated with a rare but severe side effect called intussusception, which requires surgery. The new rotavirus vaccine was just introduced in 2006, so long-term monitoring for millions of children has not yet been completed.

Measles, Mumps, and Rubella (MMR)

The MMR vaccine protects against three illnesses: *measles*, *mumps*, and *rubella* (also called German measles). Of the three, measles is the most severe with a one-in-one thousand risk of encephalitis (brain inflammation) or death. Mumps has a lower risk of serious illness although it has occasionally been associated with testicular problems and infertility in boys who contract the disease.

Rubella is a classic public health vaccine. The illness is mild and insignificant in children. However, if a pregnant mother contracts the disease, she risks having a miscarriage or severe birth defects. We immunize children less to protect them from the illness than to decrease the risk of pregnant women developing a disease which could cause serious harm to the babies they carry.

In the early 1900s, almost all children contracted these illnesses in childhood, meaning that there were millions of cases a year. Since the vaccines were introduced, the diseases have become very rare. There are usually fewer than three hundred reported cases of mumps per year in the United States. Similarly, there are usually fewer than three hundred cases of rubella and one hundred cases of measles reported per year. Thus the chances that you will be exposed to the measles, mumps, or rubella are low.

Although most side effects of the vaccine are mild—fever, rash, swollen glands—significant side effects of the vaccine can occur. Some children might have seizures (one in three thousand children) and some might develop transient low platelets that cause bleeding (one in thirty thousand). A reported risk of autism was once associated with the vaccine, but since 1998 there have been multiple large studies that have not shown any link between MMR and autism.

The recommended schedule for MMR is to give the vaccine between twelve and fifteen months of age, with a booster between ages four and six.

Varicella (Chickenpox)

Like measles, mumps, and rubella, in the early 1900s almost every child developed *chickenpox*, leading to millions of cases every year in the United States. For most children, it was a benign illness. However, at its peak, about twelve thousand people a year were hospitalized, and one hundred people per year died of complications of the illness. Most of these individuals were adults or were immunocompromised individuals who tend to develop a more severe version of chickenpox.

Given the benign nature of chickenpox for most children, it is important to recognize the public health benefits of the vaccine. If enough people are immune to the illness, it will not be able to spread far, and each outbreak will be limited. Over time, chickenpox will become like measles, mumps, and rubella, with only hundreds of cases a year instead of millions. This will mean fewer hospitalizations and fewer deaths from complications.

The varicella vaccine is effective in preventing most cases of chickenpox and making those cases that do occur milder than average, with fewer spots, lower fevers, and more rapid recovery. The majority of side effects of the vaccine are mild, including a sore arm, fever, and rash. One more serious risk that occurs in 1 in 1000 children is a seizure caused by a high fever.

The CDC's recommended schedule for Varicella as of 2006 is to give the vaccine between twelve and fifteen months of age, with a booster between ages four and six.

Hepatitis A

Hepatitis A is another virus that affects the liver. It is transmitted orally by either food or drink or by coming into contact with the stool of persons infected with hepatitis A. Although most people with hepatitis A have merely a mild flu-like illness, 20 percent of those affected are hospitalized, and three in one thousand die from complications of the illness. There are about six thousand cases of acute hepatitis A in the United States each year.

The vaccine is more than 99 percent effective and has occasional mild side effects such as a sore arm, headache, or fatigue. The vaccine is recommended for children aged twelve to twenty-three months and for travelers to countries with a high prevalence of the disease. A booster dose is recommended at least six months after the first dose.

Choosing Not to Vaccinate

We strongly encourage you to vaccinate your baby with all the recommended vaccines, but in the end, the decision is yours. Unfortunately, some doctors do not present it that way and pressure parents to vaccinate their children. You should be aware that some physicians may refuse to have your child in their care if you do not vaccinate. They feel that it is so inappropriate to not vaccinate that they do not want responsibility for caring for unvaccinated children. So, if not vaccinating or vaccinating on an alternative schedule is important to you, be sure to ask prospective doctors about their policy on having un- or under-vaccinated children in their practice. That way you won't choose a doctor only to find that her practice guidelines are incompatible with the choices you are making for your child.

If you decide against vaccinating your child, be aware that public schools and day care centers require children to be "fully vaccinated" in order to attend. The definition of "fully vaccinated" varies by state and does not necessarily include all the vaccines that appear on the recommended schedule put out by the CDC. Also, it is possible to get an exemption to some or all vaccines. There are four kinds of exemptions (though some may not be allowed in your state): medical, religious, philosophical, and proof of immunity. To find out more about these exemptions and which ones your state allows, contact either your local school district or local health department for more information.

One very important thing to remember: If you research this topic further, be aware that many books, articles, and websites have an agenda, whether it be pro- or anti-vaccination. Do not take everything stated as the absolute truth. This is one issue that you really need to be well-informed about, regardless of your decision about vaccinations. Do the research thoroughly, and keep doing it as your baby grows.

14

Sleep

Ah, sleep. The thing new parents pine for. Remember the days when you were well-rested? (We don't either.) Some parents are blessed with babies who sleep really well—whether it's for long periods of four to five hours each between wakings or whether it's all night long. And some of us are blessed with babies who wake every hour or couple of hours. Even if your baby is sleeping for long stretches, waking up at night takes some getting used to.

Honestly, there's not a lot you can do about the frequency of night wakings. There are so many factors involved with why your baby might be waking up. We'll address those in this chapter and offer ideas for how to encourage your baby to sleep longer. But we make no guarantees. (Sorry about that, but we can only do so much from this side of the page!) Sometimes all it takes is time. As baby gets older she'll sleep longer. In the meantime, we'll offer suggestions that will encourage her to fall asleep more easily and (we hope) sleep longer. We'll cover bedtime routines, the different kinds of sleeping arrangements, and talk about sleep associations and how to change them.

Keep in mind that your child will be sleeping through the night eventually. And so will you. (And, you should know that from a medical point of view, there is no problem with a baby waking several times during the night.) We'd be remiss if we didn't admit that those moments in the middle of the night with a toasty, snuggly little baby in your arms can be some of the best moments as a parent. The peace and quiet of a dark night, just the two of you awake, and you marveling that this little person knows you as "mom" or "dad" can remind you that there's actually nothing in this world that compares to being a parent.

But on to sleep . . .

Sleeping Like a Baby

One of the great challenges of parenthood is getting your baby to sleep. And to stay asleep. For a newborn, this really isn't an issue. Newborns sleep, and sleep, and then sleep some more. (Though you should keep in mind that newborn night wakings can be as often as every couple of hours because they are hungry.) Bit by bit, your baby will have more alert times and longer awake periods, which are wonderfully exciting as you get to know your little one.

Did you know that "sleeping through the night" actually means that baby sleeps for just a five-hour stretch? That's all. Nobody's talking about sleeping for eight or nine hours when they talk about babies sleeping through the night. Though that's what we'd like them to mean! If your baby sleeps for a five-hour stretch, then she is technically sleeping through the night. Eventually she will sleep longer and longer until she's sleeping for a full night. That can happen early on, or it may not happen for a couple of years, even. It all depends on your baby. Each baby is different.

So why do babies wake up at night? Well, initially it's because they're hungry. Their tiny stomachs only hold so much, and as soon as that small amount is digested they're in need of more. Remember that babies are growing at an astronomical rate. What fuels the growth? Food!

Unfortunately you cannot just stuff a baby's tummy to make her sleep longer. That doesn't really work. Babies can only take in as much as their stomachs will hold, so don't try to force your baby to eat a little more in the evenings in hopes of getting her to sleep longer. That can interfere with her natural inclination to stop eating when she's full, which is a valuable tool that can help her avoid weight issues later in life. Also, you shouldn't give her any solid food before her body is ready for it. Solids that are introduced earlier than necessary are more likely to give her food allergies than to get her to sleep all night long. Eventually she will be sleeping through the night, but remember that some things you simply cannot rush.

Babies also experience sleep cycles like we do. In fact, everybody wakes up in the middle of the night—adults and children. We all go through lighter sleep into deeper sleep, then back into lighter sleep, and then into deeper sleep again. The cycles start out short, only twenty to twenty-five minutes at first, then forty-five minutes, and then ninety minutes for the rest of the night. We all know the feeling of being woken from a deep sleep and feeling disoriented, or of being alert when waking from a light sleep. Babies experience the same thing.

Unlike adults and older children, when babies wake in the night, they are not necessarily able to just drift back to sleep like we do. They need help, and one of our jobs as parents is to provide that help. Don't worry that by helping them back to sleep through snuggling or rocking or nursing they will never learn to do it themselves. Of course they will learn to get themselves back to sleep! There are no sixteen-year-olds who cannot get themselves back to sleep. Sooner or later we all learn to do it. And when babies are ready to do it on their own, they will. (It's just like every milestone—walking, for example. When babies are ready to walk, they will walk. We cannot make them walk before they are developmentally ready. The same goes for a baby getting herself back to sleep. She'll do it on her own when she's ready.)

When helping your baby fall asleep, remember that everyone—adults and children—fall asleep to cues or to certain associations that tell us it is time to sleep. These associations help us to fall asleep when we get drowsy. One of our jobs as parents is to figure out what cues our baby is using to fall asleep. We all fall into routines of how we get our babies to sleep. You may find yourself rocking your baby to sleep for each nap and at bedtime, or perhaps you nurse your baby to sleep. Maybe you tend to walk around with your baby in your arms or in a sling to get her to drift off. These are all cues that you are using to help your baby fall asleep.

You may read articles and books that tell you not to rock your baby to sleep or not to nurse her to sleep, because then she won't be able to fall asleep without you. We're here to tell you that there is absolutely nothing wrong or bad about consistently rocking your baby to sleep, or nursing her to sleep, or walking her to sleep. As long as you are happy doing it and it works, do it!

Over time, your baby will need these cues to fall asleep. In general, whatever you do to get baby to sleep at 8 p.m. when she is first going to sleep is what you will need to do at 2 a.m. when she wakes up again. So if you rock your baby to sleep all the time, for example, she will come to expect to be rocked every time, and may have a tough time falling asleep without being rocked until she is much older. If you thoroughly enjoy rocking your baby to sleep every night, then do it. But keep in mind that if at some point you want her to fall asleep in a different manner, you'll have to change her sleep association.

She's likely to resist a change in her bedtime routine at first. (We all like our routines, don't we? So do babies). She may have trouble settling, be more fussy, or take longer to fall asleep. You'll have to decide when is a good time to start transitioning her. It's not something you should tackle when you're under stress elsewhere in your life, as it can be a bit of a difficult process. When you decide to change sleep associations or cues, *make sure you really want to change them.* Are you doing it because others are telling you to? Are you being criticized? Make sure it's what *you* want, because it will take some work. And it probably won't be easy— for you or for your baby.

To prevent your baby from having one specific sleep association, you might consider having her fall asleep in different ways. Rock her sometimes; nurse her at other times; walk around with her in a sling or your arms sometimes; lay her down when she's drowsy. That way she'll have many different ways that she can fall asleep.

When working on this issue, the question really comes down to this: What is more important *right now*—that you get some sleep or that you teach your baby to fall asleep on her own? If you are exhausted, then it may not be the best time to change a sleep association. It takes a lot of work, patience, kindness, and sleepless nights. If what you really need is sleep right now, then we suggest doing what you need to do to get that sleep. If that means you choose to keep rocking or nursing your baby to sleep, so be it. When you are better rested and have been getting reasonably good sleep for a while, then you may feel up to the challenge and ready for change. And, hey, you may not actually have to change her sleep association at all—she may one day surprise you by not wanting to be rocked to sleep. She may change it herself!

Sleep Training

If you decide that you need to train your baby to sleep through the night, (and remember that sleeping through the night is defined as sleeping five hours in a row), we encourage you to do it gently. It will probably be very hard on everyone. When considering this course of action take the whole family's interests into account. It is no more appropriate to allow the parent's needs to dominate than it is to allow the baby's needs to dominate. The baby's needs are just as important. So don't make this decision lightly if it offers only a minor convenience to mom and dad.

Before you jump straight to sleep training, take some time to figure out why your baby may be waking frequently at night. Is she uncomfortable? Does she get too hot? (Dress her in lighter clothes.) Does she get too cold? (Dress her more warmly.) Are her sleep clothes bothering her? (Try cotton if you're using polyester.) Is she very sensitive to sounds? (Try white noise to help her sleep.) A sensitivity to certain food may even be causing your baby to wake at night. There is often an underlying cause that when found and fixed will have baby sleeping much more soundly, with no need for sleep training.

However, there may be times when it is critical to change a child's sleep patterns. It might be necessary when you are exhausted and not functioning, are spending long periods away from your child, or are continually angry because of the sleep deprivation. Jamie even had one family in his practice in which the marriage was threatened because of sleep issues.

If you find yourself in a similar situation and feel the need to consider sleep training, do your research first. We recommend a specific sleep book in the Resources section at the end of this book but there are others available. Most important: Don't make a decision in the middle of the night. Such decisions are hasty and usually made in anger. It is better to have a well-thought-out plan, agreed upon by both parents, and written down so that you can refer to it if there are any questions.

It is also important to be consistent. Make sure your plan is something you can follow through on. It is worse for you and your baby to start a new sleep program only to stop it three nights later because it is too difficult. If you are not sure that you can stick to it, don't start it in the first place.

That being said, if you start out confident in your plan in theory but find that the reality of sleep training does not feel right to you (it doesn't seem like the right thing for your baby and is causing you more stress than the night wakings were), and you're thinking that you do not want to do sleep training after all, it's okay to stop. Our caution above is simply against starting and stopping again and again. That sends mixed messages to your baby, and is unfair to everyone involved.

One thing that we parents are not told enough is that babies grow out of their dependence on things. We don't actually have to teach them most new skills, they simply become independent or do things themselves when they are ready. They will not always need you to fall asleep (seriously, you're not going to be rocking your sixteen-year-old to sleep if you rock her every night as a baby), so there's no real need to rush it by pushing them to self-soothe or fall asleep on their own before they are ready to do it. When they are capable and developmentally ready, babies will learn to self-soothe and fall asleep on their own.

If it's important to you to that your baby sleeps on her own at an early age, we urge you to handle it with gentleness and kindness. Remember that your baby is a person with needs and feelings just like you. If you've put your baby down when she's drowsy and she cries, pick her up, calm her, and try again when she's calm. Repeat it over and over. It'll take some time (weeks or months possibly), but she'll learn to fall asleep on her own. At the same time, she will also learn that you'll come to her when she cries. She'll learn that you are there for her when she needs you. That's an important thing for her to know.

Back to Sleep
Always put your baby down to sleep on her back. And if your baby will be in day care—whether in your home or elsewhere—make sure that your day care provider will do the same.

Encouraging Sleep

One thing to keep in mind in the midst of all this sleep talk is the simple fact that *you cannot force a baby to fall asleep*. You may desperately want your baby to go to sleep, and you may be getting frustrated because she's up later than usual and you just need a little time to yourself. Regardless of all that, you cannot force her to fall asleep. It's impossible. And please remember during those times of frustration (and you will have them), that whatever is going on is not your baby's fault. She's not doing it on purpose; she's not staying awake or crying in order to upset you. She needs you. It's sometimes really hard to see beyond our own discomfort and empathize with our baby, but it's an incredibly important skill to master.

So, if she's not tired, do not try to get her to go to sleep. You will both just end up frustrated and upset. For those times that she is tired and ready for sleep, here are some suggestions for helping your little one sleep better and longer—so you can do the same.

Signs of Tiredness

Look for signs of tiredness, including rubbing eyes, yawning, fussing, grumpiness, getting quiet, and not wanting to play anymore. You'll become accustomed to your baby's sleep cues. When you see that she's getting tired, head for naptime or bedtime right away. Don't wait for a few more minutes so you can watch the end of your favorite TV show (or finish on the computer or finish the chapter you're reading) before you put your tired baby to sleep. You might miss the sleeping window. If you wait too long, baby may get a second wind by the time you go to put her down to sleep. Then it may take forever for her to fall asleep, or she may fuss and cry more because she's tired but not able to settle at the moment. You may miss the end of your show, but you'll save yourself and your baby a lot of frustration and stress by putting her to bed when she indicates that she's tired.

Sound Cues

Creating sound cues to tell baby that it's still nighttime can help her to fall back to sleep on her own during the night. You may want to try white noise, like a fan or air purifier (or a white noise machine itself), or play soft relaxing music (make sure it's not stimulating—a lot of classical music is) all night long. Turn on the music during your bedtime routine so baby associates it with falling asleep. Then keep it playing all night. When she stirs in the night, and is not hungry, she may learn to just fall asleep to the nighttime sounds.

Distinguish Baby's Nighttime Noises

If your baby stirs or makes a little noise in the night, don't immediately pick her up or move her into position to nurse. Not every noise during the night means baby is waking up. Wait to see if she's really waking, or if she's just making sleeping noises. You don't want to pick her up and wake her if she's actually still asleep. It'll teach her to wake up more often! If she is waking up and needs you, then attend to her right away. Don't let her cry and get worked up—it'll take longer for her to fall asleep again.

Day/Night Reversal

One thing you can easily do to help baby sleep more at night and less during the day is to distinguish day from night. When you put her down for her naps, make sure it's in a well-lit room with daytime noises. At bedtime (and all night long) she should be sleeping in a dark, quiet room. Create different routines for naps than those you use for bedtime. They can be similar, but perhaps the bedtime routine will be a little longer. (See the next section, "Creating a Peaceful Bedtime," for ideas about bedtime routines.) Do not talk or sing during nighttime feedings; you do not want her to think it's time to wake up and play. At night, only change her diaper only if it has leaked, if you think it'll leak soon, or if she's pooped. (Changing diapers at night can wake up your baby more).

Also, if your baby is sleeping for long periods during the day and waking up a lot at night, it means she has her days and nights mixed up. Try to keep her awake longer during the day: engage her, do activities together, sing, dance, whatever it takes! Encourage her to be awake more during the day, so she'll sleep for longer periods at night. Make these distinctions from the start of her life.

Why is Baby Waking Up?

If your baby has been sleeping pretty well at night, then suddenly begins waking up more often, there may be something going on. Things that might be interfering with baby's sleep include:

- Teething
- Reaching developmental milestones
- Napping too late in the day
- Being hungry because she didn't eat enough during the day
- Illness (stuffy nose or ear infection, for example)
- Allergies

Encourage Regular Naps

That being said, you also want to encourage your baby to take regular naps. If she naps well during the day, she'll sleep better at night. (We know it sounds like a paradox, but it's true.) The trick in distinguishing day from night is to eventually fall into a napping pattern of two or three naps a day that happen around the same time each day. A nap should be no longer than three hours at most. (Remember to keep the room bright. Do not darken the room for naptime.) In between those naps, baby should be awake and in the middle of whatever you are doing. Keep her active. Engage her, talk with her, play with her, tell her all about making lunch while you're making it, take her for walks, bring her along to the laundry room to do another load. Expose her to sights, sounds, and smells to stimulate her.

Creating a Peaceful Bedtime

When we get to the end of the day, the last thing we want is to have chaos or hassle. We want peace, quiet, low lights, soft sounds—things that help us relax. Creating a bedtime routine with your baby helps you achieve this for both of you. As your baby gets used to the routine, it becomes a cue to her that it's almost time to go to sleep. Her mind and body begin to prepare for that winding down process of getting ready for sleep.

What should your bedtime routine include? That's up to you. We'll suggest some things that can be part of a bedtime routine, but ultimately you have to decide for yourself what you want to do to help your child relax and get ready for sleep at the end of the day. Things you may want to consider include giving baby a bath or a massage, reading stories, playing soft music, dimming the lights, brushing teeth, snuggling in a chair or in a bed together, rocking, nursing, having a bottle, giving baby her pacifier, singing, or walking around with her in a sling. As your baby gets older you may want to include picking up her toys together and saying good night to the toys. (This will also help teach her to put her things away at the end of the day.)

We recommend that you offer a final feeding for the day sometime during the bedtime routine. In the best-case scenario you would separate the food from the sleep by several steps, such as feeding before brushing teeth. This will give baby a chance to fill her tummy right before bed and will not create a sleep association with nursing or eating to sleep. If you're happy nursing your baby to sleep every time she needs to fall asleep, do it. You should be aware that the American Dental Association warns against any food being left on baby's teeth when she's asleep—that includes breast milk. Never put a baby to bed with a bottle in her mouth because that can increase her chances of developing early childhood cavities.

Try to keep the lights low and the sounds (including your voice) soft and relaxing. Choose bedtime stories that are soothing and read them in a gentle, low voice. Now is not the time to get baby laughing and giggling—though sometimes it's difficult not to! She may be primed for fun if she gets to play in the bath, then has your undivided attention as you get her ready for bed. She'll look awfully cute and dazzle you with happy smiles. But if you get her excited it will just take longer to get her relaxed enough to fall asleep. (Okay, so give into the impulse sometimes—just not too often because you want her to associate the bedtime routine with winding down, not winding up!)

Remember that you can have as many or as few steps in your bedtime routine as you want. And the routine will change as baby grows. You might also want to create a nap time routine that is similar to the bedtime routine, but shorter. For example, your naptime routine might just be turning on quiet music, reading two stories, and then snuggling until baby falls asleep.

Sample Bedtime Routine
1. Dim the lights.
2. Put toys away and say goodnight to them.
3. Take a bath and get dressed in pajamas.
4. Give one last feeding.
5. Brush teeth.
6. Turn on nighttime music.
7. Read three stories.
8. Sing a bedtime song.
9. Snuggle until baby falls asleep.

Parents' Sleep

While we're on the topic of sleep, let's talk about how important it is for parents to get enough sleep. We know that's easier said than done (seriously—we *know*), but you will be in a better frame of mind if you get enough sleep. You will be better able to handle the ups and downs and challenges of parenting if you are at least moderately well-rested. So take a nap when baby is napping. Go to bed at 7 p.m. if baby goes to bed at that time (especially if your baby wakes often at night). Catch your sleep while you can because when you are overtired you have much less patience. And parenting, after all, is a practice in patience.

Sleep is incredibly important for parents, because we need sleep to function well. We need sleep to be able to get through the day feeling good about how we handled things. We need sleep to be able to give our best to our children day after day. Basically, we need sleep!

You will sleep again... someday. Really. It's true. We promise. But for now, know that, as with most things, it is just a matter of time. Patience, patience, patience.

> Sleep is huge when it comes to handling things calmly and having the patience to deal with a crying baby, or simply handling the stress of being a first-time parent. It may seem as though the older your child gets, the more patience you need! The key to parenting is patience. And the key to patience is sleep. So do whatever you can to get enough sleep during the day if you're sorely lacking in sleep at night.

15

Crying

Babies cry. It is an uncomfortable sound to us as parents, and it should be! A baby's cry is a sign that something is wrong. *Babies always cry for a reason*—and our job is to decipher their cries and try to right what is wrong.

Crying is a baby's first form of communication, and listening to him is your first conversation with your baby. We have some suggestions here to help you with those conversations. We'll show you different ways to soothe your baby when he cries and offer some ideas for helping *you* get through crying periods as well, including dealing with colic.

The Language of Babies

Crying is a baby's only way to communicate with you to tell you he needs something. It's baby's first language! He cannot say to you in words "I'm hungry" or "Something's wrong . . . I need your help." But that is what he's trying to tell you through his language—crying.

It's important to respond to his cries, to help him when he's asking for help. Though you may not always figure out exactly what he's trying to say, you will be helping him just by being there with him and trying to help.

Many books will tell you that you will be able to tell what your baby needs by the sound of his cry, that you will learn what his "hungry-cry" sounds like as opposed to his "lonely-cry." It's true that a baby has different sounding cries for different problems. Honestly, though, if this is your first baby, you may not be able to make that distinction—and that does *not* mean that you are a bad parent. It may take you until the second or third child before you can really distinguish between the different sounds of baby's cries. This is one of those things that comes with experience.

Why Babies Cry

As we've mentioned, babies cry to tell us that something is not right. Our job is to figure out what that something is. Most of the time you'll be able to figure it out relatively quickly by going through this list of possible causes:

- Is he hungry?
- Is he tired?
- Does he need his diaper changed?
- Is he hurt? (Has he bumped into something? Is he teething?)
- Is he uncomfortable? (Is he hot? Cold? Is something in his clothes poking him?)
- Is he bored?
- Is he lonely?
- Is he feeling overwhelmed by new people or places?
- Does he need comfort?

The reason for your baby's cry is very likely to be one of those listed above.

Sometimes babies will cry when they hear loud noises like those of a vacuum cleaner, blender, or hair dryer. If your baby cries every time you use the vacuum (or make some other loud or scary sounding noise), here's a great trick you can use. Right before you turn on the vacuum, alert him about what you are going to do. With a happy and excited demeanor, say "I'm going to make a big noise! Yay! Big noise!" Clap your hands and look really happy about it, so baby will be anticipating something wonderful. When you turn on the vacuum, continue with the "Yay! Big noise!" routine. A few instances of introducing the scary (or potentially scary) noise as a positive sound will help make it less scary for him.

Sometimes, however, babies just cry and there is no discernable reason. Perhaps he just needs the emotional release of a good cry. (We've all felt that, haven't we?) The best thing that you can do is just hold him and comfort him as best you can. Stay with him even though you may start to feel frustrated that he's still crying. He needs to cry in your loving arms to feel safe and calm again.

If your baby is crying and you're starting to get frustrated and angry, take a mental step back. Instead of focusing on your own discomfort or frustration, focus on your baby. Remember that he is unhappy or uncomfortable for a reason. Empathize with him. Realize that he's not crying on purpose to interrupt your sleep or to upset you. He's genuinely in need. When you take the focus off yourself, and place the focus back on your baby, you'll often find that your resentments and frustrations suddenly melt away.

Ways to Soothe a Crying Baby

- Hold your baby. That may be all he needs to find comfort. Studies show that babies who are held more cry less.
- Nurse your baby—it's fair to say that being at the breast is baby's favorite place, where he feels most happy.
- Go somewhere quiet if you think he might be feeling over-whelmed. Reconnecting with mom or dad in a quiet, calm space may be what he needs.

- Offer a pacifier, if you're using them. He may just need to suck.
- Interact. Sometimes babies just want someone to talk to. So find a comfortable spot to sit, look your baby in the face, and talk to each other. (Holding baby while working at the computer or surfing the Internet can be really boring for him, and he'll let you know by fussing. The cure is to move to a different spot where you can focus entirely on baby and interact with him.)
- Try white noise. While some babies are scared by loud noises, most are soothed by the fan or washing machine or radio static between stations. We've heard from parents who found that running the vacuum was the *only* way to get their baby to sleep!
- Walk, either carrying baby in your arms or in a sling or baby carrier. Try different rhythms and paces to find what works for your baby. Movement is often the best way to lull a baby to sleep.
- Dance around the room with him! Put on some funky tunes and bounce to the beat.
- Rock him. It doesn't matter if it's in a glider rocker or traditional rocker, many babies love the motion of being rocked, especially when they are snuggled against your chest.
- Sing. Choose one tune that you always sing when comforting your fussy baby or trying to get him to sleep. He'll start to associate that song with good, relaxing feelings and will immediately start to calm when he hears it. It even works in the car when baby is crying. He can be comforted (sometimes to sleep) just by the sound of your singing voice. (It'll work for a couple of years, too!)
- Drive. The classic tactic for soothing a crying, tired baby. Put him in the car seat and drive around until he's asleep.
- Go outside. Sometimes the change of scenery is soothing, as is the fresh air. Talk to your baby about what you see and hear outside. Go for a walk with baby in a sling or carrier.

- Look in a mirror. Take baby into the bathroom and see if he'll look at himself and you in the mirror. Babies love looking in mirrors! Smile and laugh with him, and talk to him about what he sees.
- Offer a teething ring or frozen teething toy if baby is cutting teeth.

Sometimes, however, you may not be able to figure it out. You may have gone through all the options and found nothing that will make your baby happy again. This can be because your baby has been crying for too long and has gotten so upset that he cannot calm down.

For example, let's say that your baby crying because he's is hungry. If you cannot get to him reasonably quickly—perhaps you're in the car and almost home, so you don't want to stop—he may get so worked up that by the time you get him out of his car seat, he's inconsolable. You offer your breast or a bottle because you're pretty sure he's hungry (it's been a few hours since you last fed him) but he doesn't latch on. He just cries. You change his diaper, but he doesn't calm down and get smiley as he usually does during a diaper change.

> Optimally, it's best to always hold a crying baby, offering him comfort and a loving presence, but if you start feeling anger that could get out of control, it's best to leave him in a safe place to cry while you take a few moments to get yourself together. Baby's safety is always the number one priority.

He just cries. You snuggle him close and walk him around the house, but he just cries. After crying and crying for a good half an hour, he finally starts to calm, and you offer your breast again. He immediately latches on and nurses hungrily. And you breathe a sigh of relief.

What you've just experienced is a baby who's gotten too worked up, too upset, and cannot calm down. That's what happens with babies if they cry for very long. They get all wound up and do not know how to wind themselves down. They need your presence and loving arms to find their way back to calm, but it usually takes a while. If this happens to you, don't give up in frustration if it seems as though nothing you do makes it any better. Just being there does make it better. Even if he's still crying. He needs you. It's just going to take him a while to calm down.

Sometimes you may find yourself getting so frustrated with your crying baby that you get really angry with him. In these instances, you need to take a physical step back. If there is any chance *at all* that you might hurt your baby (perhaps you start handling him a little roughly), gently place your baby in a safe place, like a crib, and walk away. Go into another room and gather yourself. Breathe deeply. Drink some juice. Splash water on your face. Do whatever it takes to calm *yourself* down. Then you should be better able to focus on the distress of your crying baby, rather than on your personal distress at not being able to soothe him. It's okay. He'll get through this. You'll get through this. This too shall pass.

Dealing with Colic

First, let's define colic: inconsolable crying that goes on for at least three hours a day, several days a week, for several weeks. Colic usually starts during the first few weeks of life, and it may continue for longer than three months. The crying is often worse in the evenings. This happens in babies who otherwise seem healthy and happy. About 20 percent of babies get colic.

A colicky baby may scream literally for hours, seeming to be in pain. He may bring his legs in toward his tummy, get red in the face, and be gassy. Though the gas may contribute to the problem (or may be in response to it because baby can gulp air as he cries), no one knows what really causes colic.

Colic is terribly upsetting and stressful for parents because they feel as if they must be doing something wrong if they are unable to console and calm their baby. They're not!

If the baby you've been blessed with happens to be colicky, there are some things you can do to try to help your baby and yourself. Be aware that some food intolerances can make colic worse. Dairy products, broccoli, and cauliflower are common culprits, so a breastfeeding mom might want to try eliminating these foods (and any others that cause gas) from her diet. If you are formula-feeding, you may want to switch brands to see if that helps. If you are using bottles for breast milk or formula, make sure you're using bottles and nipples that reduce the amount of air baby can swallow while feeding. Also, make sure to burp baby after every feeding.

Walk with your baby in a sling or carrier—motion often helps to calm a colicky baby. Rub his tummy or his back. Go outside with him. Take a bath together. Make sure that you (or your partner, spouse, friend, mother, or other helper) stays with him, holds him, tries to comfort him. He cannot control what is happening. He is not doing it on purpose or trying to control you. He is in desperate need of loving arms when he's colicky. Stay focused on helping your baby through this. If you start feeling frustrated and resentful, switch your focus away from your own discomfort and back to your baby and how he's feeling. (See the Tip box in the "Why Babies Cry" section in this chapter on page 202.)

It's incredibly stressful to have a crying baby that you cannot seem to soothe. So make sure that, if at all possible, you get to take breaks during the bouts of crying. Mom and dad can take turns holding him, walking with him, rubbing his tummy. Or if Grandma or other family and friends are nearby, ask for their help in caring for your baby. A break from the screaming and crying will refresh you, alleviate your frustration and stress, and help you remain empathetic toward your baby, rather than becoming so upset and resentful that you cannot calm him. Keep in mind: "This too shall pass." (This is a good phrase to have in your repertoire as a parent at all stages!) And, finally, remember that all babies eventually outgrow colic.

Crying babies, colicky or not, can be very frustrating for parents. Comfort your baby as best you can. You'll learn what comforting techniques work really well for him as you go along. You'll also learn what doesn't work. Both are very important discoveries! If you find out that a certain thing never works to comfort baby, you won't have to bother trying it out the next time and can get to a solution more quickly.

Do your best to empathize with what your baby is experiencing. Sometimes we forget to do that, or we get so wrapped up in our own experience that we are blinded to what our baby is feeling. That's okay. It's normal. When you realize that you've been overcome by your own stress, just bring your focus back to your baby and remember how much he needs you. It makes a world of difference in relieving your own frustration, and helps get your baby what he needs.

Finally, if you have concerns that your baby's prolonged crying is more than just colic, feel free to see your doctor. There are medical conditions such as esophageal reflux that can mimic colic. It will be simple for your doctor to determine if there is anything more serious going on.

Health Matters

All babies get sick. It might be a fever, a runny nose, or vomiting and diarrhea, but unless you live in a cabin in the woods and never come into contact with other people, you will face some sort of illness in your baby's first year. In fact, you will most likely face several illnesses because on average, she will be sick sixty days per year in the first two years of her life. Unfortunately, she won't be able to tell you how she is feeling, so you will have to do your best to interpret her symptoms, many of which will be discussed below. This chapter will offer you advice on the best ways to prevent these illnesses when possible, how to manage the simple ones at home when they occur and when to worry enough to call your doctor.

Top Ten Ways to Keep You and Your Baby Healthy

1. Breastfeed your baby.
Breastfeeding your baby protects her from all sorts of illnesses. These include the simple ones like runny noses, ear infections, and diarrhea, as well as more severe diseases like asthma and allergies, and even dangerous ones like diabetes, pneumonia, and even

certain types of cancer. It also lowers mom's risk of developing certain diseases like diabetes and ovarian, uterine, and breast cancers, plus it helps her lose extra baby weight more quickly, which is healthy in its own right. (Read more about the benefits of breastfeeding in Chapter Eleven.)

2. Wash your hands.

The most effective way to prevent the spread of infection is washing your hands regularly. If you use soap and water, you need to do a thorough job, lathering your hands for fifteen seconds, and being sure to get the tips of fingers, in between fingers, and the backs of your hands clean. Antibacterial soaps and special disinfectants are not necessary; hand washing alone is sufficient. You can teach young children how long it takes to wash their hands by having them sing "Happy Birthday" as they lather and then rinse their hands when the song is over. Alcohol-based hand sanitizers are just as effective as soap and more convenient, but can dry hands out more, especially in winter. We recommend that you keep several sanitizers stationed around the house and have one in the diaper bag, too. And remember, everybody, including you, should wash or sanitize their hands before touching the baby.

3. Stop smoking and avoid all cigarette smoke.

This is obvious but still merits repeating. Smokers themselves are generally sicker than nonsmokers, with a higher risk of illness, infection, heart disease, and cancer. Children who live with smokers have more ear infections, asthma, and lung infections. They are also at a higher risk for SIDS. If you smoke now, stop! If you can't stop by yourself, ask your doctor for help. If friends or relatives who smoke visit your house, please make that sure everyone—even you and your partner—always smoke outside away from your baby. If you visit someone who smokes, ask them to smoke outside while you are there, or if someone insists on smoking around your child, consider not visiting them.

4. Avoid sick people.

This is another obvious suggestion, which, unfortunately, can be amazingly hard to follow. We so want to visit our friends, to get out of the house, and to talk to other adults that we will sometimes allow ourselves to visit someone who "just has a cold." You and your baby will get sick only if you are around people who are sick. It helps if you set an example to friends and family and do not allow your baby to visit if she is under the weather. If you have to visit or receive a visit from someone who is sick (maybe the baby's grandmother who has bronchitis), make sure your baby stays more than three feet away if the sick visitor is coughing (that is the distance the droplets can fly) and have the visitor wash their hands thoroughly if they insist on holding your baby.

5. Vaccinate your baby—and yourself.

Vaccinations protect you and your baby from a variety of diseases, some of them rare but many of them common and prevalent in the community. If your baby is less than six months old, all adults who routinely come into contact with her should receive TdaP, a tetanus/diphtheria booster vaccine with a pertussis booster mixed in, as long as they have not had the tetanus booster within the last two years. In addition, during flu season, commonly defined as between October and March, those adults should also receive a flu vaccine. (Read all about vaccines in Chapter Thirteen.)

6. Make sure your baby is safe when sleeping.

The phrase "Back to sleep" is a reminder that babies should sleep on their backs to decrease their risk of SIDS. In addition, don't forget to use a firm mattress, avoid soft objects such as pillows and stuffed animals in her sleeping area, and if you are using a blanket, pull it no higher than her chest. You can tuck the blanket in on the sides if you are worried that she might shift the blanket and cover her face. Check out Chapter Four for in-depth information about safe sleeping.

7. Buckle up.

Both you and your baby should be appropriately buckled up in the car. Although more children die each year from SIDS than in motor vehicle accidents, vastly more children, and adults, are injured each year in car accidents. Your baby's car seat should be facing backward until she is weighs more than twenty pounds *and* is at least one year old. (She must meet both requirements before she can ride in a car facing forward.) If you have any concerns as to how to install the car seat in your car, find a free car seat evaluation center to show you how. You can also try your local police or fire department.

8. Cough into your elbow.

We didn't learn this trick until we were adults, but it is very effective. Most of us simply cough into open air or into our hands when we are sick. But how many of us wash our hands after each and every cough? If you cough into your elbow, the droplets are contained and you are less likely to spread illness when you touch something or someone with your hands.

9. Get enough sleep.

Make sure that you and your baby are getting enough sleep. Well-rested parents and babies are not only happier, but they are also healthier because they are better able to fight off illnesses.

10. Eat healthy foods.

Remember what your mother told you: You are what you eat. When you start solid foods after your baby is six months old, make sure you are choosing a wide variety of colorful, healthy foods for her.

Illnesses

There are numerous illnesses that your baby might experience in her first year. The rest of this chapter describes various illnesses and symptoms, explains how to manage them at home, and tells you when to contact your doctor. Beyond the specific recommendations below, it is important to follow some general rules.

First, keep your baby well hydrated. Most illnesses can lead to dehydration, whether through an associated fever or just from a baby not eating or drinking as much when she is not feeling well. Regularly offer breast milk or formula, if tolerated, or electrolyte solution (like Pedialyte® or Gatorade®) if the former is not tolerated.

Second, keep your baby close to you. She will want and need contact with you to make her feel safer and more secure. It is okay to carry her around all day long if she wants and to snuggle her to sleep for her naps. Hugs and kisses are as important as medicine in helping your baby feel better.

Fevers

A fever is a person's response to infection. The general belief is that the body is better able to fight off an infection when its temperature is higher. This might be because the virus or bacteria doesn't reproduce as well at a high temperature or because certain enzymes needed by the microbes are affected by the higher temperature. An alternative theory is that the fever is a side effect of the process of fighting off the infection. If that is the case, the fever is not particularly helping to fight the infection but just extra heat generated during the battle.

A fever is any body temperature greater than or equal to 100.4 degrees Fahrenheit or 38.0 degrees Celsius. The most accurate method of taking your baby's temperature is the rectal thermometer. Oral thermometers won't work at this age, and an axillary thermometer will merely give you an approximate temperature. The newest technology is the ear, or tympanic, thermometer, which rivals the rectal temperature for accuracy—when used correctly—and is much easier for both the baby and the parents. However, because it is difficult to use the ear thermometer correctly, especially in babies, it often gives inaccurate readings.

In general, feel free to use the axillary or ear thermometer for approximate temperatures and trust them if they report a fever. However, if you want to know the exact temperature, the rectal thermometer is best. For less than $15.00, you can buy a reputable, multi-purpose thermometer that can be used for axillary, oral, and rectal temperatures (simply change the plastic sleeve after each use). If you still have any thermometers containing mercury in your house, dispose of them in the hazardous waste center in your area. They are considered dangerous because if broken they can leak mercury, a very toxic substance.

In the first two months of your baby life, you must call your doctor if your baby has any fever at all. Very young babies are particularly susceptible to infections. Fevers can be very dangerous for newborns, so physicians are extra careful about evaluating them. The evaluation might include blood work, X-rays, and even a spinal tap. If there is any concern that a serious infection is present, your baby may be admitted to the hospital and given IV antibiotics for a few days while the doctor waits

How to Take a Rectal Temperature

1. Put the plastic sleeve over the probe of your digital thermometer.
2. Dab some petroleum jelly on the end of the probe.
3. Separate the buttocks and insert the tip of the thermometer into the rectum. If there is not an indicator line on the thermometer, insert it no more than one inch.
4. Leave the thermometer there until it beeps, and then read the temperature.
5. Discard the plastic sleeve and wash your hands.

for lab tests to show if any bacteria are present in the blood stream or spinal fluid.

After the first two months, however, a fever is usually just a clue that your baby is sick. Sometimes you will need to see your doctor to find out where the infection is hiding or what bacteria or virus is responsible. You should be extra careful if your baby has a rash with the fever, is not eating or sleeping well, or has a high fever (over 102 degrees Fahrenheit or 39 degrees Celsius). You should also consider calling your doctor if your baby has a fever that doesn't come down with fever-reducing medicine, if she is less than six months old, or if she was born premature. You should also trust your parental instincts and see the doctor if you think that she is sicker than you would expect given her temperature, or if she is lethargic or difficult to rouse.

There are many helpful clues to tell you how sick your child really is. (This will become second nature to you with time and experience.) Children who are still active and alert are generally doing better than those who are collapsed on your shoulder. Children who are eating, drinking, peeing, and pooping well are usually less sick, and the same is true for babies who don't seem to be in pain or distress despite the fever. An ear infection hurts, and pneumonia makes it hard to breathe. You'll notice changes in your baby, and over time you will develop a sense that tells you when something is wrong.

Treating a fever is simple. First of all, if your baby does not seem uncomfortable with the fever, you may just let it run its course. Do not bundle up your baby in layers of warm clothes— that will only make her body temperature go up. Keep her lightly dressed to help her stay cool. To get her fever to come down quickly, put your baby in a bath. Make sure the water temperature is lukewarm but not cool. You don't want to chill her; you just want to use the water to transfer heat away from her body.

As for medications, acetaminophen and ibuprofen work well. Ibuprofen lasts longer, and in our experience is better at bringing down high fevers, but acetaminophen is easier on the stomach. If your baby has any kind of stomach discomfort, such as vomiting or diarrhea, then acetaminophen is the better choice.

The simplest way to give your baby medicine is to place the liquid into her cheek and let her swallow it. If you place it too far back in her mouth, she might gag and spit it up.

An alternative is to put it in her bottle, if she is taking bottles. We suggest you put the medicine in just a small amount of liquid. If the medicine is mixed into her full four-ounce feeding but she only takes two ounces, you won't know how much medicine she ingests. If you mix the medicine into just an ounce of breast milk, formula, or juice instead, she is more likely to take all of it and you can be certain she has gotten the full dose of medicine.

Finally, if she is taking solids, it is also possible to mix the medicine into her food. Before doing this, make sure your doctor or pharmacist says that it is appropriate to give this particular medicine with food. Some medicines are to be given only on an empty stomach. Acetaminophen can be given with food, and the manufacturers of ibuprofen actually encourage you to take it on a full stomach.

If the fever persists after one dose of medicine, it is possible to alternate acetaminophen and ibuprofen every three hours. For example, if you gave a dose of acetaminophen at 10 a.m. but your baby still has a fever at noon, you could give her a dose of ibuprofen at 1 p.m. The next dose of acetaminophen would come at 4 p.m., then ibuprofen at 7 p.m. and so on. Some experts don't feel alternating medicines is a good idea because there are no studies indicating that two medicines alleviate the fever any better than just one, but many parents find this pattern very effective. Some experts also worry about safety because the instructions can be confusing, but if you are careful and attentive, you will give each medicine only four times a day so there will be no chance of an overdose. If you are uncertain about any of this, don't hesitate to consult your doctor before giving your baby any medicine.

Breathing Problems

Most respiratory illnesses are mild and can be managed at home, but some breathing issues are very serious. Fortunately, the symptoms in these instances are quite clear. A baby who is having problems breathing will be anxious, uncomfortable, and in some distress. She will not be able to calm down or relax because she is working so hard to breathe.

She will also be breathing faster than normal. The normal breathing rate for newborns is around forty to fifty breaths per minute, whereas for older children it is thirty to forty breaths per minute. Thus, any rate higher than sixty breaths a minute is a cause for concern. Be sure to count your baby's breaths for an entire minute, because children often have irregular breathing patterns.

If she is putting a lot of effort into breathing, breathing hard like a runner at the end of a long race, and lifting her shoulders to breathe, then you should be concerned. In addition, if her color looks blue or dusky, that is a sign of breathing troubles.

Finally, you might see nasal flaring or retractions when your baby has some distress with breathing. Nasal flaring occurs when the openings of

Signs of Breathing Distress
- Baby is breathing faster—sixty breaths or more a minute. (Count how many breaths she takes for a full minute to be sure you get an accurate number.)
- She is working hard to breathe.
- Baby is flaring her nose with each inhale.
- The skin at the base of her neck or on her ribs sucks in with each inhale.
- Baby's color is blue or dusky.
- She is acting anxious and uncomfortable, and cannot relax.

If your baby is showing any of these signs, call your doctor immediately.

the nose dilate (open wider) to allow more air to enter the lungs. Retractions occur when the skin on her chest or at the base of her neck sucks in with an inhale; you will see this between the ribs or just behind the collar bones. Not all retractions are signs of distress, though. Retractions at the junction between the bottom of the ribs and the abdomen can be normal and if they are the only ones, might not signal a concern.

If your baby has any of these signs of breathing distress, call your doctor right away and discuss the situation with him. Your baby may need to be evaluated immediately, even in the middle of the night.

Coughs and Croup

Fortunately, most coughs are not dangerous. They occur intermittently during the day, don't cause any distress, and go away on their own. However, you should know that a cough is often the last symptom to disappear after an illness. One study found that 25 percent of coughs last for more than a month after the end of the illness! So if your baby has recovered nicely from the cold with the runny nose and fever but still has a lingering cough for several weeks, you don't necessarily need to worry. Feel free to see your doctor for reassurance (after all, baby's so little!), but don't be surprised if he simply says she has a post-infection cough.

Another common illness that leads to a cough is *croup*. Croup is caused by a virus that infects the upper airways (as opposed to a pneumonia, which affects the lower airways and lungs). The virus causes swelling of the trachea and larynx which creates the classic hoarse cry and barking cough that characterizes croup. The cough sounds a lot like the bark of a seal.

Croup is worst at night, but the severe symptoms usually last only one to three nights. Interestingly, both a steamy bathroom and cold night air can be helpful in treating the cough. In the former case, just turn on a hot shower, let the steam fill the room, then sit in the steamy bathroom with your baby. (Jamie has even slept in the bathroom with a croupy kid.) As for the using the cold night air, remember to bundle her up before you take your baby outside.

You can also run a vaporizer or humidifier in her room at night for mild croup. If the symptoms don't resolve with these simple measures and your baby seems in more distress (as described above in the previous section on breathing problems), you should contact your doctor and be ready to go to the nearest emergency room or urgent care center for treatment.

Many parents will notice that their babies calm down and breathe normally on the way to the ER, probably due to breathing in the cool night air. If she is significantly better with no distress, feel free to turn around and go home as you have already treated her appropriately. Of course, if she is still having worrisome symptoms, get to the hospital to have her evaluated.

Colds

On average, your baby will get six to nine illnesses per year in the first two years of life. Most of them will be respiratory infections, which result in a cough, runny nose, and low-grade fever. As mentioned earlier, if she is not acting particularly sick, is eating and drinking well, and the cough is not too bothersome, you can usually manage this at home. Many parents find that "steam cleaning" their baby helps. This means either using a vaporizer or humidifier in her bedroom or sitting with her in a steamy bathroom. Some parents even create a mist tent by placing a cool mist vaporizer under a table and a tarp on top to hold the mist in. They then climb under the tarp with their baby, allowing her to breathe in the mist in an enclosed space. (If you use a warm mist vaporizer, be sure to keep baby away from the vaporizer because it does get dangerously hot—both the device as well as the steam coming out of it.)

There are many over-the-counter remedies for mild upper respiratory infections. They include medicines for cough, congestion, and runny noses. While these medicines are generally safe, randomized studies have not shown them to be at all effective, despite the fact that some parents swear by them. In addition, there have been cases of overdosing when parents used two over-the-counter remedies and didn't realize that the ingredients over-lapped. So the current recommendations are to not give any over-the-counter medicines to children less than two years of age. Consult your doctor first if you think your baby may need medica-tion for her cold.

Vomiting and Diarrhea

One of the least pleasant aspects of parenting is dealing with vom-iting from a stomach virus. We're not talking about spitting up, which is simply the gentle regurgitation of some breast milk or formula. This is vomiting, the forceful expulsion of stomach con-tents. It spreads farther, smells worse, and is just plain yucky. For-tunately, most vomiting lasts only twelve to twenty-four hours. It can be repetitive and you might see over ten bouts of vomiting in that time frame, but it will go away relatively quickly. Because it almost always goes away on its own, you rarely need medicine or IV hydration, just time. If you are concerned, however, give your doctor's office a call to find out whether you should take your baby in for a visit.

Unlike vomiting, diarrhea can commonly last for more than a week. Here we're talking about watery stools, not just mushy ones. There might be five to ten stools a day or just one or two. The explosive nature and watery consistency can be a chore to clean up and also cause a rash on your baby's bottom. If she expe-riences a rash, a thick, protective diaper ointment, along the lines of zinc oxide, will help protect her sensitive bottom. (Don't be stingy with the diaper rash cream; spread it on thick to help pro-tect her sore bottom.)

The major concern with vomiting and diarrhea is the possibility of dehydration. With so much liquid going out of baby's body, she can easily become dehydrated. There are several clues to tell you if she is: A dehydrated baby does not shed tears when she cries and has a very dry mouth. She does not urinate as much, and her diapers are dryer when she does go. She will be less active and, in the worst-case scenario, may become listless.

The first rule for treating dehydration is to continue to nurse your baby if you are breastfeeding. Breast milk is extraordinarily well absorbed and tolerated. If she continues to vomit while taking breast milk or if you are not nursing, then you want offer an electrolyte solution like Pedialyte®, Gatorade®, or Recharge®. These solutions are better than water because they replace needed electrolytes.

When replacing fluids, you should offer frequent small sips to your baby. One to two teaspoons (or 5 to 10 ml) every five minutes will give her 2 to 4 oz of liquid every hour. If she is able to tolerate that, you are more than adequately replacing the fluids lost. Even if she vomits a few minutes after drinking some fluids, she has probably kept some down. It is amazing how quickly fluids are absorbed and how well this oral rehydration works.

If she continues to vomit and shows signs of being significantly dehydrated, call

Homemade Rehydrating Drink

Store-bought electrolyte solutions can be expensive, but you can easily make one yourself at home, with ingredients that you are likely to have on hand (and for a fraction of the cost!).

Mix together:
- 8 cups of water
- 8 tablespoons of sugar
- 1 teaspoon of salt
- 1 teaspoon of baking soda
- 1 packet of unsweetened Kool-Aid (optional)

Make it fresh only when you need it, and keep it in the refrigerator. When baby no longer needs it, throw out what's left as it won't keep.

your doctor. Your baby may need IV fluids, which are usually given in the emergency room and can quickly rehydrate her.

Constipation

Most of the time, what parents perceive as constipation is actually not constipation at all. True constipation is the painful excretion of hard stools, similar to the consistency of rabbit droppings. If you can easily indent a stool with your finger, your baby is not constipated. And not having a bowel movement for several days is not constipation. Many babies have no bowel movements for several days and then have a large, explosive—but soft—poop. Babies can have seven stools in a day or one stool every seven days; both of those patterns can be normal.

If your baby has skipped several days of bowel movements, what matters is how uncomfortable she is. If she is not bothered by the buildup of stools, then you don't need to do anything. However, many parents report that their baby is more uncomfort-

Signs of Dehydration
- Baby is not active, and may even be listless or lethargic.
- Baby has no tears when she cries.
- Her mouth is dry.
- Baby has fewer than three wet diapers per day.

If your baby is showing these symptoms, please call your doctor right away.

able than usual until she has a poop, and is then content again. With those children, it helps to stimulate a bowel movement to prevent the discomfort. You can do this by massaging her tummy, bicycling her legs, or using some rectal stimulation with an over-the-counter glycerin suppository or the tip of a thermometer. For both of these methods, use petroleum jelly and don't insert the suppository or thermometer more than one inch into the rectum.

True constipation almost never happens in exclusively breastfed babies. However, if you are bottle-feeding your baby and she is actually constipated, you may find that her hard stools are painful for her and cause some bleeding around her anus. In this situation you will want to soften her stools. Depending on how old she is, you might add fluid or fiber to her diet. If she is more than six months old, apple juice is a wonderful option to consider in addition to her regular feedings because it loosens the stools and also adds some liquid. Many parents add several drops of dark cooking syrup to their baby's bottle and adjust the dose until the stools come out soft. This method supposedly absorbs water into the colon and makes the stool looser. Finally, if none of these simple measures work, your doctor can prescribe some safe medicines that can soften the stool.

Ear Infections

Babies are prone to getting middle ear infections because they have so many colds over the first two years of life and also because they have narrow eustachian tubes. The eustachian tubes connect the middle ear to the back of the nasal cavity. They serve the dual function of draining fluid from the middle ear and equalizing pressure between the middle ear and the surrounding environment. When the narrow eustachian tube is blocked or collapsed by the swelling from a cold, fluid can't drain and pressure can't equalize. If bacteria or a virus grows in the fluid, that will increase the pressure and push on the tympanic membrane, or eardrum. That increased pressure is what causes the pain your baby feels during an ear infection.

There are several clues that may suggest that your baby has an ear infection. First, she might have a fever, though it is possible to have an ear infection without a fever. Next, she might be cranky during the day or wake up more frequently in the middle of the night, though that can also be from teething. Finally, she might pull on her ears, though many babies pull on their ears because they are fun to play with. In the end, the best way to determine if there is an infection is to have your doctor look inside the ear.

The most important treatment for middle ear infections is pain medicine. Use regular doses of acetaminophen or ibuprofen for the first forty-eight hours. Doctors used to think that all middle ear infections required antibiotics; but recent studies have shown that about 85 percent of these infections will resolve on their own without antibiotics. The American Academy of Pediatrics (AAP) has recently published a guideline as to when to treat an ear infection with antibiotics and when to wait.

The guideline recommends that children under six months of age be treated with antibiotics because they are so little and are more vulnerable when dealing with infections. The suggested treatment for a middle ear infection in children between six months and two years of age is either immediate antibiotics or delayed antibiotics. Delayed antibiotics means watchful waiting and starting antibiotics in two days if the child is not improved. Over age two, the recommendation for most children is delayed antibiotics.

Crusty Eyes and Blocked Tear Ducts

Many babies are born with watery eyes that turn crusty after sleep. This is usually caused by a blocked tear duct. The tear duct drains tears from the inner eye to the nose (which is why you get a runny nose when you cry). If your baby has a blocked tear duct on one or both sides, it won't be painful, but she will be unable to drain her tears normally, and she will get material buildup in her eyes. After your baby sleeps for several hours, the duct will become crusty and matted, and the buildup will need to be wiped away when she wakes up. (It can even "glue" her eyes shut while she sleeps.) You can clean baby's eye by wetting a wash cloth with warm water, then gently wiping the crust away. If her eyes are crusted shut, you may need to hold the warm wash cloth to her eye for a few seconds to soften the buildup first, and then wipe. Do not press on her eye; just let the wash cloth lay on it.

The treatment for blocked tear ducts is massage, warm compresses, and time. A gentle massage between the nose and the corner of the eye will often unclog the duct and allow it to drain. Blockage may recur in the same or opposite eye but more massage or warm compresses will usually help. Over time, the ducts will grow and become less narrow and less likely to clog. If the problem persists after your baby is a year old, there is a simple, outpatient duct dilation surgical procedure that can be done to permanently fix the problem.

Pink Eye

If your baby has pink eye, or *conjunctivitis*, the white of her eye will be bloodshot. There are several dangerous causes of pink eye, such as iritis or glaucoma, and thankfully most of these causes have a few obvious symptoms. The most important of these symptoms are pain and photophobia (fear of bright lights), which means that your baby's eye will hurt and she won't want to open her eyes in sunlight or a bright room. If your baby has pink eye but is sitting there happily, looking around the room without distress, she does not have a dangerous kind of pink eye.

The remaining, more innocuous causes of pink eye are allergies, a viral infection, or a bacterial infection. Allergies usually involve both eyes, whereas infections usually involve just one eye at first, followed by an infection in the second eye. Most infections (some specialists say over 95 percent) are viral and do not require antibiotics. As with the middle ear infections discussed earlier, a common treatment pattern is to only use antibiotic drops if the conjunctivitis has not cleared within a couple of days. Call your doctor if your baby's eyes are still bloodshot after two or three days. Whether the conjunctivitis is viral or bacterial, it is very contagious so be sure to wash your hands whenever you are caring for your baby.

Baby Rashes

Most rashes in babies fall under the category of "benign baby rashes." They are transient and never cause a problem. Some examples of this type of rash are baby acne, milia (little white dots on the nose), and heat rashes (blotchy, flat red spots in areas of skin that were too warm).

Another common rash that is usually minor is a diaper rash. Your baby's bottom will look red and sore, sometimes only in the creases or around the anus, but in some cases covering the whole diaper area. Most diaper rashes are caused by irritation or heat, and will clear up with time and the use of over-the-counter diaper ointments. Remember to really slather the ointment on to help protect baby's bottom so it can heal. You also might want to air out your baby's bottom by letting her play without a diaper for a while (on a waterproof pad of course or outside during the summer!).

Occasionally, however, a fungal infection will occur in the diaper area. This yeast infection is brighter red and angrier looking than most diaper rashes and won't go away with regular diaper rash cream. In addition, you will notice small red "satellite lesions" at the edges of the rash as it grows outward. You'll need to take your baby in to see your doctor if you suspect she has a yeast rash because it requires a prescription antifungal cream to clear up.

Cradle cap, or *seborrheic dermatitis*, is an unsightly but benign condition that involves dry flaky skin along the scalp, forehead, eyebrows, and eyelashes. It tends to be most noticeable on the scalp because most babies have very little hair. There is no required treatment for the rash; it will go away on its own over several months and does not bother the baby. If you want to remove it for cosmetic purposes, a touch of olive oil will lift the scales off the scalp but won't treat the inflammation. If you want a more permanent solution, tar-based shampoos have proved helpful for many parents by treating the underlying inflammation. These shampoos smell terrible, but they work great and are safe for children.

Thrush

Thrush is a fungal infection on the surface of the mouth, usually the tongue and inner cheeks. You will see white material that is difficult to scrape off. Not all white material is thrush, and not all thrush needs to be treated. (Your doctor will be able to determine this.) If your baby is not bothered by the thrush and you are not noticing any pain with breastfeeding, then you don't need to treat it. If you decide to treat thrush, your doctor will prescribe a simple antifungal liquid that can be painted on baby's tongue and cheeks for several days. (Read more about thrush treatment for breastfeeding mother-infant pairs in Chapter Eleven.)

Stay Home or Go Back to Work?

To work or not to work? That is the question. For a lot of people, it's not an option to stay home with their baby; they must work to support their families. For those who have the luxury of choice, it is not always an easy decision. Trying to figure out what they want to do and what will be best for the family can be stressful.

Staying home is hard work. Going back to work is hard work. (Being a parent is hard work!) Both options offer different benefits and drawbacks. This is a personal decision *and* a family decision. It impacts everyone: baby, mom, and dad. So it's worth taking the time to consider the pros and cons of either decision if you are one of the many who struggle with this issue.

If you have the option to work or stay at home, ask yourself what will make you happiest. It may seem selfish to focus on yourself and not on your baby, but it's not. A happier parent is a better parent. An unhappy parent shares those feelings of resentment with their baby. Make yourself, and your family, as happy as possible by making the best possible choice for yourself.

Staying Home

A top reason for staying home is the benefit to your baby of having his mom or dad as his primary caregiver. Your child will be more attached to you, and you will have the benefit of knowing him better—which makes many aspects of parenting easier. You will know what works and what doesn't work. You may have fewer frustrations in parenting him because of this attachment and your intimate knowledge of your child.

You will also be there for all of his firsts—the first time he smiles, the first time he rolls over, the first time he sits up by himself, crawls, or pulls himself up to standing, his first steps. It's exciting to be there, regardless of whether baby is your first child or your fifth. Raising your child is the most important thing you will do in your lifetime. It is the toughest job there is, but also by far the most rewarding.

Benefits
- You and your baby are together.
- You get to be there for all of your baby's firsts.
- You develop a strong bond with your baby.
- You get to know your baby really well.
- You do not have to find someone else that you trust to take care of your baby every day or worry that your baby is not being well taken care of.
- You do not have to pay for day care.
- Staying home is more conducive to exclusive breastfeeding.

Drawbacks
- You may feel isolated, especially if you don't get out to meet other adults.
- You may miss the camaraderie you have when you work with others.

- You may miss the work you once did or the sense of accomplishment it gave you.
- Your family will make less money.

Stay-At-Home Dads

Another question to consider is: Who will stay home? Mom or dad? Traditionally, mom has done most of the caretaking, but babies are reaping the great benefits of their dads being more involved, being more in tune, and being more available to them. More and more men are taking time off from work to stay home with their babies. Staying home can be just as rewarding for dads as it is for moms. We know some wonderful fathers who are staying home with their children. They are incredibly attuned to their child's every move and mood, and are happy, thoughtful parents.

Having dad more involved in child care overall is wonderful because children need time with both parents! Dads play just as important a role as moms do, and they are just as capable of being nurturing parents to their children as moms are. The more involved dad is, the more confidence he will have in his ability to take care of his kids, and the more confidence he will have in his ability to nurture.

You can find a lot of support for stay-at-home dads on the Internet. A great place to start is at www.slowlane.com. It has articles, resources, and links to dads' groups and information.

Surviving Staying Home

Staying home is hard work. You may feel as if you are constantly working, whether it is caring for your baby, doing laundry, washing dishes, cleaning the house, paying bills, or cooking meals. It's more than a full-time job. It's a twenty-four-hour job because you're always either on duty or on call. Parenting offers no time off on weekends or holidays, and no paid vacations. It can sometimes feel overwhelming, especially to first-time parents.

Whether you're feeling overwhelmed or not, consider the following suggestions to help you keep your sanity.

Try hiring a mother's helper or babysitter to give you a break on a regular basis.

A mother's helper is a student or an adult who watches your child for you in your home while you are at home doing something else. You may need the break just to catch up on household chores, to get some uninterrupted time on the computer, to make dinner, or even just to take a shower. Or if you work from home (work that garners a pay check), a mother's helper can be a great way to get work done while staying home with your baby. Jen hired a mother's helper two and a half years ago to look after her first son while she was working on another project. (She kept her second son, who was three months old at the time, with her while she wrote). The project ended, but the mother's helper didn't! Jen so appreciated having time to get things done—writing or household work—that she's continued having her mother's helper come every week.

Think about hiring a mother's helper on a weekly basis, if you can, or even a bi-weekly or monthly basis. They also make great babysitters! Because your child already knows and loves this person, it will make it easier to leave him with the caregiver for a couple of hours at another time. Additionally, during her time in your home, your mother's helper observes how you comfort your child, understands how you handle discipline, and knows the house rules (for instance, what you allow and do not allow your child to do). That is a huge benefit for the babysitter, your child, and you.

Be kind to your baby and realize that he needs to get to know someone and feel comfortable with her first before you leave him in her care. (This will take more than just an extra fifteen minutes before you leave.) If you will be leaving your baby with a sitter, then have the sitter come over to your house to get to know your baby a week or two before she is to come sit, if possible. Have her spend some time with your baby (with you there). It may take very little time before your baby is saying "Mom who?" after your sitter arrives. Or it may take more time. It just depends on your child's personality.

Once your baby is comfortable being cared for by the sitter, you will be able to leave your baby in her hands, knowing that he's unlikely to cry much or feel stressed because you've left him. He'll be in the arms of another loving caregiver with whom he is familiar. You'll reap the benefits of this trust by being able to fully enjoy your time away without having to worry about him.

Get help from your partner.
Stay-at-home parents are always working or on call, and this 24/7 job requirement is a recipe for burnout. You will need breaks to be able to handle parenting issues with calm, kindness, and empathy, so partners need to pitch in—whether that means caring for the baby or doing the dishes. Talk with your partner about your new roles as parents, especially what it means practically, how you can make each other feel appreciated, and how you can help each other. Ask for help when you need it. Most adults failed Mind Reading 101 in high school. Your partner will not be able to know telepathically every time you need help, so speak up about it!

One way your partner can help every day is by spending time with your baby as soon as he or she gets home from work. If a parent is working outside the home, then baby's been without him or her all day long and he's going to need to reconnect with that parent. This will also give the stay-at-home mom or dad some downtime.

Take breaks.
It is amazing what a difference it makes to be off duty, even for the twenty minutes you need to take a shower. You can go into

the shower feeling burnt out and overwhelmed; twenty minutes later you can exit the bathroom feeling refreshed and ready to handle anything again. Maybe you'd like to have a half hour to yourself to read a few chapters of your current book or a magazine in peace. Or perhaps you need to go for a walk or a jog. Make an effort to do whatever recharges you on a regular basis with your partner's help.

Get out of the house regularly.
Find playgroups in your area and try them out until you find one that best fits you and your baby. Go to playgrounds or parks to meet other parents. Go to children's museums. Go shopping! The bright colors and activities of the grocery store or mall can entertain your baby while you shop. And you might even find a minute to read a magazine at the local bookstore's café. Have lunch with a friend. Stroll through your local art museum or aquarium. Baby will love the sights and sounds—all the stimulation. And you'll love the contact with the world outside your home!

See if your area has a regular free newspaper highlighting parent and child resources. Read it to find listings of activities for young children and go. Ask your library if they have a weekly story hour for infants and toddlers. If you meet some other parents that you really like, form your own playgroup! Getting out and being with other parents is a great way to keep your sanity. You can commiserate about parenting issues, ask advice, and learn from each other. These parents become a part of your network of support, and the socialization benefits both you and your baby.

Also, consider taking a class or doing some activity on a weekly basis. You may even choose a class for you and your baby to take together—there are music classes, tumbling/gymnastic classes and the like. (Many of these "classes" are much like playgroups, though usually there are fees involved.) Or maybe take a class without baby. Get out and do something just for you, whether it is learning to make pottery, taking a yoga class, or joining a local community chorus—whatever interests you. Getting out on your own periodically can do wonders.

Finally, realize that staying at home doesn't mean that you'll always be at home. As your child grows, you will have more opportunities to get back out there. When he starts school you'll have time for a part-time job, if you want. Or perhaps you'll opt to go back to a full-time job and find care for him in the afternoons after school. It's not a life sentence. And if you come to the conclusion, after being home for a few months, that it just isn't working, you're unhappy and feeling lost without your job, you can always change your mind. One of the best things you can do for your baby is to find a way to be happy. If that means going back to work, then that's what you should do.

Working

For many people, working actually makes them better parents. They are happier going to work and are therefore happier coming home from work. Some people do not thrive on being stay-at-home parents, and that's okay. It's important to know yourself and know what will help you be your best for your child. For some, that means going to work.

There are many reasons why going back to work is a good decision for some parents. There is certainly a benefit for the family finances if both parents are working. Plus, working gives you the opportunity to be out amongst your colleagues. Adult conversation never sounded so good! You are intellectually stimulated and able to focus on things beyond your family. You may feel better and find that you are more creative when you have a working identity in addition to being a parent.

You'll experience a big change in your routine when you get home from work. Instead of being able to relax or take care of the housework, you're going to find your arms full of a little person who is delighted to see you and needs to have your undivided attention for most of the evening. What he needs is his mommy and daddy fix. He's been without you all day long—his favorite people in the world—and he's going to need to reconnect with you when you get home. The best thing you can do is to focus on your child. Hold him, carry him, read with him, play with him. Spend quality time with him for the remaining hours that he is awake. Once he's gone to bed, you can take the time to fold the clothes, do the dishes, and check your e-mail. Or mom and dad can take turns in the evening. While mom is playing with baby, dad can figure out what to make for dinner. After dinner, mom can do the dishes, while dad gives baby a bath and puts him to sleep.

Benefits
- Your family makes more money.
- You get time for yourself.
- It's fulfilling, and you have a separate identity from being a parent.
- You benefit from the social aspect of working with others, getting regular adult interaction and conversation.
- It's intellectually stimulating.
- You get a break from the constant child care routine at home.
- It's easier to schedule appointments for yourself—you can do them during work hours while baby is being cared for.
- Your baby will get used to having different caregivers and will be more flexible.
- If you breastfeed, you will be pumping, which means your partner can do nighttime feedings part of the time with a bottle of pumped breast milk.

Drawbacks
- You may feel guilty.
- You will not get to spend as much time with your baby.

- You may miss many of his firsts.
- You will have to pay for day care.
- You will have to pump if you are breastfeeding.
- You may have to stop breastfeeding (or choose to only nurse at night when you are home) if your job does not make it possible for you to pump during the day.
- You have to find someone you trust to care for your baby.
- You cannot allow your baby to work out his own schedule—the workday sets the schedule.

Working Options

If you decide that you will be going back to work, but still feel sad that you will be missing time with your baby, consider reducing your hours or working part-time, if that's an option for you financially and okay with your employer. (And you will never know if you don't ask!) The other option to explore is whether you could work from home. Do you have the type of job that would accommodate that? Would your employer be willing to have you work from home part-time or even exclusively? (Again, it's worth asking.)

Working from home presents its own challenges, though. Be sure to really think about whether you can work from home. Will you have to work specific hours of the day, or can you do it whenever you want? Will you be able to focus only on the task at hand while you are working? You will probably need to hire someone to help care for your baby while you're working at home, as well. (See the first suggestion about hiring a mother's helper in the "Surviving Staying Home" section on page 232 in this chapter.)

Surviving Going Back to Work

Going back to work is hard. You will be constantly taking care of your baby when you are home, so going to work may feel like you're getting a break—except that you have to work during that break! Combining the responsibilities of home with the responsibilities of work can sometimes feel overwhelming. Add to that feeling guilty, and oh boy, you have the makings for a stressed-out parent. Here are a few suggestions to help you "work" through it all.

Get over the guilt.

Yes, you are going to feel guilty. You're going to wonder if you're doing the right thing. Every drawback of going back to work is tied to guilt in some way. But you know what? All parents feel guilty some of the time. It's not a feeling you would escape as a stay-at-home mom or dad. It's best to acknowledge the guilt, realize that you're doing the best you can with what you have, plan how you could do better, and move on. It's easier said than done, but it's a healthy goal to work toward. Don't beat yourself up over things. You have to do what is right for you and your family. If going back to work means you will be happy, then that's great! Your child deserves a happy mom and dad.

Get help from your spouse.

If both of you are working, both of you also need to be taking part in the child care and housework at home. Have a conversation with your spouse about how you two can make things work together. Take into consideration that your baby is going to need time and attention when he is awake. You might try making a game plan for how to get things done in the evenings, such as taking turns caring for baby and getting things done in the house like making dinner and doing dishes. Try to figure out how you can make each other feel appreciated, and how you can help each other. Don't expect your spouse to be able to read your mind or know every time you could use help. Ask for it! Remember that parenting is a partnership. Family is a group activity.

Connect with your baby.

Find ways to reconnect with your baby when you get home after work. Play with him; read to him; simply sit and talk with him; go for a walk with him. Focus on him. Soak in his smiles, relish his velvety soft skin, and kiss his perfect little toes when you change his diaper. Be fully present with him. Make a solid connection and rekindle your relationship with your child every single day.

Do not give in because you feel guilty.
Some working parents have a hard time enforcing the rules at home. When you have limited time with your child, you may give in because (a) you feel guilty about being at work during the day, (b) you do not want to be the bad guy or (c) you do not want to spend your time arguing or making your child unhappy. It's an understandable reaction, but it sets a bad precedent. If you give in to your child on rules or limitations that you have set (and that are reasonable and important to you), then you're working your way toward behavioral problems in the future when you actually do want to enforce those rules. In order for rules to work, you must be consistent. If, however, you've decided that a rule is unreasonable and doesn't really matter, then that's fine. Break it.

Breastfeeding and Pumping

For many moms, even if they can't be with baby during the day, their breast milk can. As we've mentioned, giving your baby breast milk is one of the best ways to keep protecting him from illness and maintaining his health. In order to do this while you are working, you'll have to have a job that will offer a quiet, clean place to pump regularly throughout the day. (If you have your own office, then you're all set. Remember to put a privacy sign on the door while you pump, though.) If you need to, explain to your boss the benefits of breast milk for your baby and for your job; a healthier baby means you will miss fewer days of work tending to a sick child.

If you will be able to pump at work, arm yourself with an efficient pump. Ask friends for recommendations, go online or consult consumer products publications to read product reviews, call your local La Leche League leader, or ask your doctor or the lactation consultant at the hospital. If you have a friend with a pump, ask to borrow hers (either to try out or to use indefinitely if your friend isn't currently using it).

Start pumping and storing your milk at least a month before you head back to work. You always want to have at least a week's supply in the freezer, and preferably more, so try to pump every day, if you can. Once you return to work you may not be able to pump enough to keep up with demand and may need to dig into your supply, so a larger stockpile is better.

Most moms find it convenient to store breast milk in two to three ounce bags that are easily available in stores or on the Internet. Don't forget to label the bags with the date the milk was pumped. You'll also want to start introducing the bottle to your baby around four to six weeks of age to get him used to drinking from it. (For more information on storing breast milk and introducing bottles, see Chapter Eleven.)

Because you will no longer be nursing your baby throughout the day, you may find that your milk supply goes down a bit, even though you are pumping. That's because baby is the best stimulant for producing breast milk. Just keep nursing when you are home, and pumping when you are at work. Try to pump on your days off too—once a day if possible—to help keep up your production and your frozen supply.

Finding Good Day Care

It is incredibly stressful, and sometimes feels like a daunting task, to try to find someone to care for your baby. No one is going to love your baby exactly the way you do. But you can find some wonderful people out there who will give your baby a lot of thoughtful, loving attention and who will take very good care of him.

First of all, you need to be at peace with the fact that no one else is going to care about your child as much as you do. No one else is going to know your child as well, or love your child as deeply, but you can still find someone who will do things similarly. You will have to find a balance between the requests you make on behalf of your child and your caregiver's way of doing things—even simple things like wanting a caregiver to heat up your baby's pumped breast milk or formula. They may give cold bottles to babies if warming bottles is not something they routinely take the time to do.

You have options when it comes to day care. There are, of course, big day care centers, small in-home day cares, family day care, and you can even hire someone to come to your house to care for your child while you are at work. If you can afford it, having someone come to your home to take care of your child is a wonderful option for a young baby. Your child will have one-on-one time with a loving caregiver who is able to focus entirely on him. You will have more control over how your child is cared for (you can require warm bottles, have your child carried more often, get lots of books read to him, have him put down for a nap according to his schedule, for example). There is certainly more socialization at an in-home or day care center, but that does not become important until your child is older.

How do you find a caregiver? Ask around. Just like finding the right doctor, finding the right caregiver is a process. Ask your friends with kids, ask your physician, members of your congregation, a local La Leche League leader, or place an ad in the paper or post flyers at local businesses (like the grocery store or natural food store). You should be able to come up with a list of good options.

What should you look for in a day care provider? Well, that's really up to you. What's important to you in a caregiver? Essentially you are finding another "parent" for your child, so you will want someone who is in-line with your parenting style and ideals.

> **Back to Sleep**
> **Make sure that your day care provider will always put your baby down to sleep on his back to reduce his risk of SIDS.**

Come up with a list of questions to ask your prospective care-givers, based on your parenting preferences. See the suggestions below for some ideas.

Interview Questions for Prospective Caregivers or Day Care Centers

1. How do you handle crying babies? How do you comfort them?
2. Do you think an infant can be spoiled?
3. What is your experience with caring for babies and young children? How long have you been doing this? Do you have children? How old are they?
4. What is the ratio of caregivers to babies/children?
5. What are the rules for sick kids?
6. Are you certified in child/infant CPR? Can I see your certificate?
7. How flexible are the hours?
8. Do you smoke? (No smokers around baby! Even if a caregiver smokes outside, it is still not a good idea.)
9. Do you always put babies down to sleep on their backs?

If you will be placing your child in an in-home day care or a day care center, then visit, visit, visit. Observe how the caregivers interact with, comfort, and discipline the children. Are they treating every baby and child with respect? Are they treating them like people with legitimate needs and feelings? Do they seem to enjoy being around and caring for children? Take a look around. Is the day care clean? Is there an order to the toys and books? Do the children seem happy and relaxed? Are the caregivers happy and relaxed? Are they patient, warm, nurturing? Find out if the caregivers are trained in CPR, as well, and what their protocols are for emergencies such as injuries and fires. A very important thing to ask yourself is whether this is a place you would want to spend time. Would you be happy here?

Ask your questions freely. Remember that you are interviewing people to take care of *your* baby. If someone seems put off by all your questions, then move on to the next day care option on your list.

Finally, realize that you have the right to change your mind. If you find that you are not as happy as you presumed you'd be by going back to work, if you are pining for your child and truly wishing you could be home with him instead, then leave your job and stay home with your child, if that's possible. Staying home doesn't have to be forever. Your child will be starting school in a few years, and you'll be able to get back into the working world then if you choose. You will only have this opportunity to be with him when he's this little once. If you find that staying home turns out to be what you really want to do, then do it. Whatever it is that will make you a happy parent is what you should be doing. Your baby will be so much better off in life and in your care if you are happy with your life—whatever it looks like.

Resources

Recommended Books

Baby Bargains by Denise and Alan Fields. A great resource for figuring out what to buy and how to save money. Includes safety ratings and reviews of baby products like strollers and car seats.

Your Amazing Newborn by Marshall and Phyllis Klaus. This short book describes in words and pictures amazing and unsuspected abilities in newborns in the first few days of life.

The Ultimate Breastfeeding Book of Answers by Jack Newman, M.D. and Teresa Pitman. A comprehensive guide to breastfeeding, chock full of great information.

So That's What They're for! Breastfeeding Basics by Janet Tamaro. A light-hearted, entertaining, and informative book.

The No-Cry Sleep Solution by Elizabeth Pantley. Detailed suggestions for solving sleep issues, and gently helping your child sleep longer at night. Includes sleep training in a kinder form.

Super Baby Food by Ruth Yaron. Wonderful guide to feeding your baby a healthy diet and making your own baby food.

Recommended Websites

Birth
Doulas of North America
http://www.dona.org

Breastfeeding:
http://www.breastfeedingonline.com

http://www.kellymom.com

La Leche League—http://www.lalecheleague.org/

LLL leaders are trained and experienced moms who breastfed their babies and may have gone through whatever problems you are calling them about. You can find leaders in your area by looking in the phone book or getting a list of local leaders from their website shown above. It's a wonderful organization of moms helping moms. LLL leaders are very willing and eager to help as best they can.

The National Women's Health Information Center

http://www.4woman.gov/Breastfeeding/index.cfm

World Health Organization (WHO) breastfeeding recommendations

http://www.who.int/nutrition/topics/infantfeeding_recommendation/en/index.html

American Academy of Pediatrics
http://www.aap.org/

Circumcision policy statement—PEDIATRICS Vol. 103 No. 3 March 1999, pp. 686-693

http://aappolicy.aappublications.org/cgi/content/full/pediatrics%3b103/3/686

Sleep guidelines—PEDIATRICS Vol. 116 No. 5 November 2005, pp. 1245-1255

http://aappolicy.aappublications.org/cgi/content/full/pediatrics;116/5/1245

Breastfeeding guidelines—PEDIATRICS Vol. 115 No. 2 February 2005, pp. 496-506

http://aappolicy.aappublications.org/cgi/content/full/pediatrics;115/2/496

Ear infection guidelines—PEDIATRICS Vol. 113 No. 5 May 2004, pp. 1451-1465

http://aappolicy.aappublications.org/cgi/content/full/pediatrics;113/5/1451

The safety of medications while nursing

These are a couple of well-respected sites where you can research the risks of certain drugs in breast milk. You can enter the name of the drug in question and find a summary of the risks.

LactMed

http://toxnet.nlm.nih.gov/cgi-bin/sis/htmlgen?LACT

Motherisk

http://www.motherisk.org/women/index.jsp

World Health Organization growth curves

http://www.who.int/childgrowth/en/

Center for Disease Control recommended vaccine schedule

http://www.cdc.gov/nip/recs/child-schedule.htm.

Stay-at-home dads

http://www.slowlane.com

National Highway Transportation Safety Administration

Car seat safety reviews:

http://www.nhtsa.dot.gov/CPS/CSSRating/

List of car seat inspection stations by zip code:
http://www.nhtsa.dot.gov/CPS/CPSFitting/Index.cfm

Researching baby products (strollers, car seats, etc.)
http://www.consumerreports.org
http://www.consumersearch.com

National Association of Diaper Services
http://www.diapernet.org

Index

G

H

I

J

R

S

Y

About the Authors

Jen Meyers, an author, editor, and mom of three amazing little people, is also a professional artist who draws naturalistic portraits in pencil. She is married to her love, Stevan, and together they are gently raising their three boys in upstate New York.

Jamie Loehr, M.D., has practiced as a family physician in Rochester and Ithaca, NY, for the past seventeen years. Although he provides a wide range of care, his first loves remain pediatrics and obstetrics. In this way he ends up caring for babies from the first prenatal visit through birth, infancy, toddlerhood, and on up. His focus is on caring for the whole family, helping to guide new parents through the ups and downs of those first years, offering his own experiences as a father when advice is sought. Jamie is married to his wonderful and supportive wife, Caitlin, and they are the parents of four young children, ages ranging from two to eleven.